A Second Adam

A Second Adam

GARTH RATCLIFFE

ATHENA PRESS
LONDON

A SECOND ADAM
Copyright © Garth Ratcliffe 2008

ISBN: 978 1 84748 450 5

Every effort has been made to trace the copyright holders
of works quoted within this book and obtain permission.
The publisher apologises for any omission and is happy
to make necessary changes in subsequent print runs.

First published 2008 by
ATHENA PRESS
Queen's House, 2 Holly Road
Twickenham TW1 4EG
United Kingdom

Printed for Athena Press

Contents

*All Bible quotations are from
the New International Version*

Foreword

If the Church is to reconnect effectively with our culture, it needs to embrace a confidence in the gospel, a renewed love for the world it serves and a thirst for the renewing work of the Spirit. Rooted in the first chapter of 2 Peter, this timely book addresses each of these issues. It will serve well all those seeking to go deeper in their faith – both Christian leaders seeking to disciple others, and those whose journey of faith has perhaps become rather tired. Throughout the book, a helpful variety of illustrations, quotations and lines from hymnody serve to refuel the readers' passion for the gospel.

Like all good teachers, Garth Ratcliffe seeks to share those truths which have served to awaken a living passion in his own heart. I warmly commend this book; it will refresh and renew the faith of all who read it.

John Samways (Team Rector, Keynsham)

Preface

Is it all a Fairy Story?

The main purpose of this book is to explore the idea of Christ, the Second Adam, who came to rescue and remake us, and our response to his saving initiative. Before I can do this, I think it is necessary to discuss briefly in this preface whether there are reasonable grounds for believing that the Christian faith is true in the first place. Evelyn Waugh tackles this question in his novel *Brideshead Revisited*. It includes a conversation between two young Oxford students, Charles Ryder and Sebastian Flyte, who are the chief characters of the story. Charles, an agnostic, questions Sebastian about his faith:

> 'I suppose they try and make you believe an awful lot of nonsense?'
> 'Is it nonsense? I wish it were. It sometimes sounds terribly sensible to me.'
> 'But my dear Sebastian, you can't seriously believe it all.'
> 'Can't I?'
> 'I mean about Christmas and the star and the three Kings and the ox and the ass.'
> 'Oh yes, I believe that. It's a lovely idea.'
> 'But you can't believe things because they're a lovely idea.'
> 'But I do. That's how I believe.'

The points at issue here are, firstly, whether Sebastian is being rather naive and, secondly, whether or not there are sufficient grounds for an intelligent person to assent to the basic propositions of the Christian faith. These propositions are that Jesus was the Son of God who came to earth to rescue the human race from sin and death, and that in doing so he was crucified, died, was buried and that he came back to life bodily. There is no difficulty in believing that Jesus was crucified. Such things happened. But it is asking rather a lot of us to believe that he was the Son of God who came back from the dead.

Probably most people would agree that there is absolutely no point in believing in the Resurrection of Christ just because we would like it to be true or because it's a warm and comforting thing to believe.

We should believe it, if we are to believe it at all, because we have reason to think that it is true. Fairy stories and make-believe are fun – but it is very dangerous to base life's major decisions on them. Our faith must not be wishful thinking. Many writers have gently mocked those who believe in and preach a life of perfect bliss in the hereafter. George Orwell created a character in his book *Animal Farm* called Moses, a tame raven, who told the oppressed animals that when they died they would go to Sugarcandy Mountain in the skies, where life would be endless bliss.

> The pigs had an even harder struggle to counteract the lies put about by Moses, the tame raven. Moses, who was Mr Jones's especial pet, was a spy and a tale-bearer, but he was also a clever talker. He claimed to know the existence of a mysterious country called Sugarcandy Mountain, to which all animals went when they died. It was situated somewhere up in the sky, a little distance beyond the clouds, Moses said.
>
> In Sugarcandy Mountain it was Sunday seven days a week, clover was in season all the year round, and lump sugar and linseed cake grew on the hedges. The animals hated Moses because he told tales and did not work, but some of them believed in Sugarcandy Mountain, and the pigs had to argue very hard to persuade them that there was no such place.

Orwell was making the same point as Karl Marx, that social oppressors often use religion as an opiate to dull the senses of the downtrodden masses – by promising them future happiness in heaven.

The poet Rupert Brooke wrote an amusing poem in which he pictures fish creating their own imaginary future paradise. Whether he is gently mocking the idea of heaven is not clear.

> Fish (fly-replete, in depth of June,
> Dawdling away their wat'ry noon)
> Ponder deep wisdom, dark or clear,
> Each secret fishy hope or fear.

Fish say, they have their Stream and Pond;
But is there anything Beyond?
This life cannot be All, they swear,
For how unpleasant, if it were!
One may not doubt that, somehow, Good
Shall come of Water and of Mud;
And, sure, the reverent eye must see
A purpose in Liquidity.
We darkly know, by Faith we cry,
The future is not Wholly Dry.
Mud unto mud! – Death eddies near –
Not here the appointed End, not here!
But somewhere, beyond Space and Time,
Is wetter water, slimier slime!
And there (they trust) there swimmeth One
Who swam ere rivers were begun,
Immense, of fishy form and mind,
Squamous, omnipotent, and kind;
And under that Almighty Fin,
The littlest fish may enter in.
Oh! never fly conceals a hook,
Fish say, in the Eternal Brook,
But more than mundane weeds are there,
And mud, celestially fair;
Fat caterpillars drift around,
And Paradisal grubs are found;
Unfading moths, immortal flies,
And the worm that never dies.
And in that Heaven of all their wish,
There shall be no more land, say fish.

'Heaven', 1913

The lines, 'This life cannot be All, they swear, / For how unpleasant, if it were!' reminds us that believing something to be true, just because we would like it to be true, does not actually make it true. We need to know that there are sound reasons for believing in something.

Some writers have claimed that faith must be blind –

otherwise it is not faith at all but sight. I disagree and wish to draw a clear distinction (as we have done elsewhere when looking at faith) between intellectual assent and trust. Intellectual assent is the acceptance by our minds that something is actually true. Trust is placing our personal confidence in something that we have already accepted as true. Trust is taking intellectual assent a step further – into commitment. Take the example of the disciples when Jesus appeared to them after his death. According to the Gospels, this was not about blind faith. They actually saw Christ, spoke to him, ate with him. They had all the evidence they needed that he was alive. Faith, for them, was to put their trust fully in the Jesus they saw. They knew him to be alive after death because their senses told them so. Even Thomas had enough evidence. He had the word of the other disciples but, possibly because he was confused and numbed by grief, he could not accept the word of his friends that they had seen Christ – but once he had tangible proof, he too believed.

So where do we stand on this matter today? We have not even seen Christ in the flesh, let alone seen him risen from the dead. Is there any good reason we should swallow the story that Jesus came back to life after the crucifixion? The Archbishop of Canterbury, Rowan Williams, was asked in a TV interview why he believed in the bodily appearances of Jesus after the crucifixion. He replied, 'Because people saw him'. The Archbishop highlighted the most important point at issue. Did the disciples really have contact with Jesus after his death? Did they see him, touch him, talk with him and eat with him?

My intention in this chapter is not to attempt any knock-down proof of the Resurrection. I am trying to explain why there are good reasons to believe that Jesus really did come back to life. I take as my starting block that which is generally accepted by the majority of New Testament scholars, whether or not they believe in a physical resurrection. This includes matters of authorship and dating of New Testament books. For the purpose of this chapter, I make the assumption that where there is a consensus among scholars, their scholarship is sound. Readers may wish to check on my assumptions. They can do this by looking at a large number of New Testament commentaries which are available in academic libraries.

The evidence that Jesus was seen by his disciples after his death is based on two sets of writings which were written in the first century AD and which much later became part of the New Testament. They are:

1. The first letter of Paul to the Corinthians
2. The Gospels and the Acts of the Apostles.

The first question we have to ask is if we have a reliable text of these works, or if the original has been so distorted by copying over the years that we no longer know what it said. A distinguished scholar, J A T Robinson, has argued the technical reasons for believing that the copies we have today are substantially accurate in their transmission.

He wrote in his book *Can we trust the New Testament?*:

> Transmission, even by word of mouth, was a much more exact and controlled process than it is for us, with teachers trained and instructed by their masters to memorise their words and pass them on with an astonishing degree of accuracy. Then the scribe, who was a professional, was much more like the modern copy typist or proofreader than the amateur playing a game. We can recognise – and so discount – the kind of errors that frequently recur...
>
> Our biggest safeguard however is the many-stranded cord of transmission.
>
> In the case of some ancient authors everything literally hangs on the thread of a single manuscript. In the case of the New Testament there are hundreds and indeed thousands of threads – and of course correspondingly numerous variations. Naturally, some threads are much older and more valuable than others – and most of the variations frankly insignificant...
>
> The wealth of manuscripts, and above all the narrow interval of time between the writing and earliest extant copies, make it [the New Testament] by far the best attested text of any ancient writing in the world. In the case of Greek and Latin classical literature it is not at all uncommon for there to be two or three manuscripts only and a gap of anything up to a thousand years. In the case of the New Testament there are, as I said, literally hundreds of witnesses, and in no case is the interval more than three hundred years and in many parts now a good deal less. In

fact one papyrus fragment of St John's Gospel stands so close to the time of writing as actually to have ruled out some of the later (and in any case wilder) dates proposed for its composition.

Another problem is the reliability of the so-called witnesses. Were they not all followers of Christ and therefore all one-sided? It is true that all the first-century claims about the Resurrection appearances of Jesus come from those who were loyal to him. This is because they were the only witnesses. This does not necessarily make their accounts unreliable or distorted. Our information about many historical events often comes from those who shared the same set of beliefs. For example, many of the events in Hitler's bunker in April 1945 were observed only by people sympathetic to Nazism. We have to be careful when we analyse what they reported, but it does not mean that we cannot come to a reasoned and reasonable conclusion about what actually happened. Of course we have to ask questions about the reliability and truthfulness of those who claim to be witnesses. That is part of all historical analysis. Those involved in writing the accounts of the Resurrection appearances made little attempt to produce a polished finished work. Although it is clear they often knew of each other's writings and borrowed freely from each other, no serious attempt was made to harmonise their writing. Had the writers been deliberately untruthful, we might have expected more harmony and polish.

It is also important to note that the writers on several occasions stress that they are well aware of the importance of reliability and truthfulness. For example, Luke's Gospel begins:

Many have undertaken to draw up an account of the things that have been fulfilled among us, just as they were handed down to us by those who from the first were eyewitnesses and servants of the word. Therefore, since I myself have carefully investigated everything from the beginning, it seemed good also to me to write an orderly account for you, most excellent Theophilus, so that you may know the certainty of the things you have been taught.

Luke 1:1–4

The writers of the New Testament understood only too well that it mattered very much if what they were claiming was actually true. It is interesting to see how they went about presenting their material.

The earliest-written claims that Jesus appeared alive to his followers after his crucifixion are to be found in Paul's first letter to the Corinthians.

> For what I received I passed on to you as of first importance; that Christ died for our sins according to the Scriptures, that he was buried, that he was raised on the third day according to the Scriptures, and that he appeared to Peter, and then to the Twelve. After that, he appeared to more than five hundred of the brothers at the same time, most of whom are still living, though some have fallen asleep. Then he appeared to James, then to all the Apostles, and last of all he appeared to me also, as to one abnormally born.

1 Corinthians 15:3–8

Paul had not known Jesus personally, but it is clear from other passages in his letter to the Galatian Christians that he knew Peter and other senior Apostles. Paul lists the appearances of Jesus (after his Resurrection) to Peter and other Apostles. He claimed that some appearances were to groups of people and some to individuals. This indicates that he believed the appearances to be actual and not visionary. This is because visions are subjective and would not be shared by groups. The last appearance, to Paul himself, seems to be in a class of its own. According to Acts, Paul saw and heard Jesus speaking. Those who were with Paul heard a sound but could not hear what was said. They saw light but could not see the person of Jesus.

It is generally accepted by scholars that Paul was writing this letter roughly twenty-five years after the death of Jesus. Most would agree that Paul sincerely believed that what he wrote was true. In other words, Paul was making a serious attempt to give information about events that would have occurred well within the time period in which people would remember accurately both the outline and the detail of what had happened. Paul points out that he is simply *reminding* the readers of information that he had already given to them some years before. He also states that he is well aware that the issue of accuracy is of vital importance. He goes on to say:

> If Christ has not been raised, your faith is futile … If only for this life we have hope in Christ, we are to be pitied more than all men.

> 1 Corinthians 15:17, 19

It could be argued that Paul was simply raising the stakes here and applying emotional pressure, but the overwhelming reaction of scholars (whether or not they believe in the Resurrection) is to accept that Paul was sincere in making these claims. This leaves us asking, was Paul somehow mistaken?

It is clear from Paul's letter to the Galatians (Galatians 2) that Paul knew Peter in particular, but also James and John, the Church leaders in Jerusalem. When he listed the appearances of Jesus, Paul was repeating the claims of the immediate disciples of Jesus. Were they themselves mistaken? Were they deliberately dishonest? Did they remember accurately? With regard to memory, I accept that no recall is absolutely perfect. However, as far as the appearances of Jesus are concerned in 1 Corinthians 15, we are looking at a time gap of less than twenty-five years. Many people alive in Britain today can remember a great deal of detail about their experiences in the Second World War. This is now more than sixty years in the past. The Queen has spoken of her experience of mingling with the London crowds with her sister and a small group of officers on the evening of VE day in May 1945. The writer of this book remembers events of thirty and forty years ago well enough to know whether important things did or did not happen. Peter, James and John would have been able to remember very well whether they saw Jesus alive after his death. We must, of course, ask ourselves whether they were being deliberately dishonest.

There are two strong arguments against this possibility. Firstly, these men led a body of people who produced the writings of the New Testament. These writings demand of us the highest possible standards of integrity and truthfulness. They urged the early Christians to be completely honest in all their dealings, even when it was inconvenient for them to do so. In this they were only following the Jewish tradition of complete personal integrity so strongly emphasised in the Hebrew Scriptures. Secondly, from all that we can gather from history and tradition, this body of people and the Apostles who led them were prepared to lose their lives, sometimes most cruelly, rather than deny their faith in Christ crucified and risen. It is true that people will die for a cause or person they believe in, but to suffer and die for something they know to be a fabrication is another matter. It is difficult to imagine that a group of people would be prepared to face unpleasant deaths for proclaiming something which they knew to be false.

But is there another possibility? Maybe the Apostles sincerely believed that they had met Christ alive after his death, and were mistaken. Perhaps they suffered from hallucinations, or even the effects of drug taking. As mentioned earlier, the problem with hallucinations is that they occur in the mind of an individual person who pictures an event subjectively. The event is not an objective reality. A group of people, whether or not they were taking drugs, do not have the same hallucinations. Both Paul and the Gospel writers claim that Jesus was seen after his death by both individual people *and* groups of people.

Although most New Testament scholars accept that the Apostles were not guilty of deliberate deceit, some scholars do not accept the Resurrection as an event of history. They argue that the Apostles were mistaken, or that the early Church gradually created the stories of the Resurrection to explain some deep conviction that Jesus was still alive – possibly resulting from some subjective experiences of the disciples. The argument is that the appearances of Jesus mentioned in the earliest writing (i.e. 1 Corinthians 15) were visions and not literal appearances. They argue that by the time the Gospels were written, second- and third-generation Christians had created stories of Jesus talking to and eating with his disciples after his death. This, they claim, was a way of rationalising the earlier visionary experiences.

One of the problems with this argument is that in 1 Corinthians 15, Paul lists a series of appearances of Jesus which includes his appearances to groups of people. As I have already argued, this indicates that Paul intended his readers to understand that the appearances were objective realities. Groups do not share subjective visions. The reason why the body of Jesus could be seen objectively by groups of people is that the body of Jesus had been literally raised.

A M Ramsey, a former Archbishop of Canterbury, argues in his book *The Resurrection of Christ*:

> The words of the tradition, as Paul reproduces it, seem incomprehensible unless they mean that the body of Jesus was raised up.
>
> > how that Christ died ... and that he was buried ... and that He hath been raised up again on the third day.
>
> Died – buried – raised: the words are used very strangely unless they mean that what was buried was raised up. What otherwise is the point of the reference to the burial? In default of the very strongest evidence that Paul meant something different and was using words in a most unnatural way, the sentence must refer to a raising up of the body.

The claim of 1 Corinthians 15 is that the body of Jesus was dead, buried, raised up again on the third day and seen.

But what are we to make of the accounts of the four Gospels? The earliest Gospel is probably that of Mark. It is generally accepted to be written in the mid-60s AD which is about thirty-five years after the crucifixion. Mark (along with the other three Gospels) tells how the disciples found the tomb empty on the first day of the week – but ends at that point. (The problem with Mark is that most early manuscripts omit the second half of the last chapter [Mark 16:9–20] – making this section unreliable evidence coming from a later date.) Matthew, Luke and John go on to claim that Jesus appeared several times to his disciples over a period of about six weeks. They claim that on these occasions Jesus had conversations with his disciples and invited them to touch him. In Luke's Gospel, Jesus eats food with them to demonstrate that he is not a ghost (Luke 24:36–49).

Furthermore, the writer of the book of Acts, who is generally accepted to also be the writer of Luke's Gospel, claims that Jesus ate and drank with the disciples after his Resurrection. Luke may or may not be the physician friend of Paul. Clearly, if he is, the link with Paul is important, because we already know from Paul's letters about the very early claims of the Apostles to have seen Christ.

The dating of the Gospels and the book of Acts is difficult and controversial. A minority of scholars, such as J A T Robinson, have argued for an early dating of all the Gospels and claimed that they were all written by AD 70. The majority go for a later dating.

In any case, the consensus of New Testament scholarship, which dates Luke's Gospel and Acts in the 70s and 80s AD, and John's Gospel in the 90s AD, means that these accounts of the Resurrection appearances were written down within the lifetime of some of the disciples. It is important to note that although it is true that average life expectancy was far lower then than it is now, we know that many people lived into what, today, we regard as old age.

The crucifixion of Jesus is usually dated between AD 29 and AD 34. The time gap between the writing of the latest Gospel and the death of Jesus is comparable with the length of time which has passed between today and VE day. As mentioned earlier, the Queen remembers vividly her VE day experiences to this day. It is interesting to note how much detail people can remember of the events of World War II and their own personal experiences of that period. The writer of Luke and Acts goes out of his way to stress how careful he has been to get his information right (Luke 1:1–4; Acts 1:1–4). If the consensus of scholars is correct, then the claims of Luke that Jesus ate and drank with his disciples after the Resurrection (Luke 24:41–43 and Acts 10:41) would have been written after a time gap equivalent to the gap between the present day and the 1950s and 1960s. Many of us have very clear and detailed memories of those years. Just imagine telling the Queen that she cannot remember in detail the events of Coronation Day in June 1953, or her wedding day in 1947!

In the same way, we would expect the disciples to remember clearly the events of the crucifixion period until their dying day. I repeat that the Gospels were written within the lifetime of some of the disciples, and the letters of Paul were written within twenty-five years of Jesus' death. The time gap is not long enough for the creation of fictitious stories by well-meaning second- or third-generation Christians. I also repeat that many people today remember the events of the 1940s and even earlier in clear detail. On top of this, they have accurate information about even earlier periods of the twentieth century from parents, friends and relatives. For example, conversations between the Queen Mother and the Queen about events between 1915 and 1935 would be based on accurate memory. These conversations would have occurred until the Queen Mother's death in 2002.

If Paul was right and Jesus did appear to the disciples, then the details of eating, drinking and conversation with Jesus are exactly the details we would expect them to remember and to remember vividly.

Some have suggested that the followers of Jesus were so taken in by his claims to be the promised Messiah that the Resurrection was *invented* by the Christians to demonstrate that he was the promised one. As Tom Wright has forcefully argued in his book, *The Resurrection of the Son of God*, this simply does not fit at all with the expectation of the Jews of the time. The idea of a personal resurrection was simply not on their Messianic calendar at all. If anything, claiming that Jesus had risen from the dead would make it more difficult for religious Jews at the time to accept Jesus as Messiah.

There are of course other possibilities. Clearly, one possibility is that Jesus never actually died, but somehow survived the crucifixion. Did Jesus really die? Did he sink into unconsciousness on the cross and then revive some time after his supposedly dead body was removed from the cross? The Gospels tell us that Jesus was scourged first and then crucified. He was put on the cross at nine o'clock in the morning and died at about three o'clock in the afternoon. The religious authorities asked the Romans to remove the bodies before evening. The two men crucified with Jesus were still alive, so the soldiers broke their legs. The reason for this is that crucifixion kills people by asphyxiation. The crucified person needs to keep shifting position in order to breathe, which needs the support of the legs. When the legs are broken, this can no longer happen and the victim dies.

The soldiers did not break the legs of Jesus – because he was already dead.

John's account says that one of the soldiers thrust a spear into the side of Jesus, and out came water and blood (John 19:33–35). It is also difficult to imagine how Jesus could have avoided asphyxiation if he had slumped unconscious on the cross. Besides this, people do not survive a combination of scourging and crucifixion and then walk around very much alive two or three days later.

So we are left with the big question – did the Resurrection of Jesus happen? Did Jesus walk about, eat food and make conversation with people after his crucifixion, death and burial? Medical science tells us that such things cannot happen. Some would claim that because they cannot happen, they did not happen. From the point of view of the New Testament, one of the most important things about the Resurrection is that it was, in a sense, impossible. The New Testament writers were well aware that people did not just rise from the dead. They knew that it was impossible – unless, of course, Jesus really was someone very special, who had powers which were greater than the forces of nature, so that he had power over death. To these people, the very fact that the Resurrection was impossible, and yet somehow happened, was a clear sign to them that Jesus was who he claimed to be: the Son of God.

We have to follow our own minds on this and reach our own conclusions, but it is important that we give the matter considerable and serious thought. Of course, it is not enough simply to accept the Resurrection of Jesus as a fact of history. If Jesus really did rise from the dead, we need to make our own all the benefits of his death and Resurrection. We need to know by faith the risen Lord. We need to learn to walk in obedience to his truth and we need to marvel at the greatness of his saving love. One poet, perhaps more than any other, has captured this sense of joy and wonder at the Resurrection of Christ. George Herbert's poem, 'I got me flowers to straw Thy way', has moved millions of men and women.

> I got me flowers to straw Thy way,
> I got me boughs off many a tree;

But Thou wast up by break of day,
And brought'st Thy sweets along with Thee.

The sunne arising in the East,
Though he give light, and th' East perfume,
If they should offer to contest
With Thy arising, they presume.

Can there be any day but this,
Though many sunnes to shine endeavour?
We count three hundred, but we misse:
There is but one, and that one ever.

Questions for Discussion

1. Why do many Christians think that it is a matter of great importance to determine whether or not the appearances of Jesus after the crucifixion were an objective historical event?

2. What, in your opinion, are the critical factors in determining if these alleged appearances were objective realities?

I

The Second Adam and the Hope of Glory

We have seen in the Preface how the Apostle Paul, towards the end of his first letter to the Corinthians, discusses some of the evidence for the Resurrection of Christ. In the same letter he goes on to write at some length about the implications of the Resurrection for us. He introduces the idea of Christ coming into this world as a new Adam who will create a new race out of fallen humanity, a race completely redeemed from sin and death and remade in his own likeness.

> The first man was of the dust of the earth, the second man from heaven. As was the earthly man, so are those who are of the earth; and as is the man from heaven, so also are those who are of heaven. And just as we have borne the likeness of the earthly man, so shall we bear the likeness of the man from heaven.
>
> 1 Corinthians 15:47–49

John Henry Newman, in his hymn 'Praise to the Holiest in the Height', took up Paul's theme when he wrote:

> O loving wisdom of our God!
> When all was sin and shame,
> A second Adam to the fight,
> And to the rescue came.
>
> O wisest love! that flesh and blood
> Which did in Adam fail,
> Should strive afresh against the foe,
> Should strive and should prevail.

According to Paul, the first man, Adam, failed to resist evil. The second Adam, Christ, defeated evil. The new, or second Adam, was to be the prototype of a new humanity recreated from the old in his likeness. Others, including Martin Luther, have also developed this idea. They called Jesus the 'proper man'. By this they meant that Jesus was a true human being. He lived perfectly – as God had intended us all to live – without selfishness and sin. He was unfallen, unspoiled and showed us what humanity was meant to be. He fought on our behalf against all the forces of evil, and he alone completely defeated them. He was the proper or real man. He was what we were meant to be and, by his grace, will one day become. Luther's great hymn 'A mighty fortress is our God' takes up this theme.

> The ancient prince of hell
> Is risen with purpose fell.
> On earth is not his fellow.
> But for us fights the proper man
> Whom God himself has bidden.

An illustration which some have found helpful is taken from the period of the Second World War. Perhaps the darkest and bleakest time in this conflict, as far as Europe was concerned, was the late autumn of 1941. Almost the whole of the continent lay under the feet of one of the most evil regimes in human history. Nazi tyranny was oppressing hundreds of millions of people. Russia appeared to be on the brink of defeat. Britain was gasping for its breath, just holding on, but totally unable to turn the tide of war and retrieve the loss of Europe to Nazism. The Allies were incapable of winning the war. Then, suddenly, the whole scene changed. In December 1941, the Japanese attacked Pearl Harbor and Germany unexpectedly declared war on the United States. Churchill's reaction was one of relief. He wrote, 'I went to bed and slept the sleep of the saved and thankful.'

It's not hard to see why. A situation of no hope turned into one of confidence that eventually Nazism would be defeated and destroyed. A weak situation became one, potentially, of enormous strength. American manpower and materials would eventually turn the tide of war. Final victory was well-nigh certain – albeit at a frightening and terrible cost, and only after very heavy losses for months and months to come.

Spiritually there may be a parallel here with something that happened, according to the New Testament, 2,000 years ago. The world lay in the grip of evil and darkness. The human race was fallen and lost. Human beings had no power to release themselves. They were in slavery to sin. They were helpless to do anything about it. They could not redeem themselves and they were without hope. Then, on a particular day in history, God sent Christ into the world that we might be saved. He sent him to rescue us from the dominion of darkness and to transfer us to the kingdom of his Son. He sent Christ to redeem us at the price of his blood. He sent him to die for the forgiveness of sins. In Paul's words:

> ...he has rescued us from the dominion of darkness and brought us into the kingdom of the Son he loves, in whom we have redemption, the forgiveness of sins.

Colossians 1:13–14

Just as the arrival of the United States into World War II brought all the immense resources of the New World to redress the balance of power in the old, so all the resources of God and of heaven were sent for our rescue in the person of Christ – the proper man, the second Adam. He lived a perfect life and resisted all temptation. He healed the sick and fought against evil wherever he found it. He shed his blood on the cross to redeem us from evil and for our forgiveness. He defeated death itself, and he shares with his redeemed and forgiven people his Resurrection and his life. Because of Christ's coming we, like Churchill, can sleep the sleep of the saved and of the thankful. And this war which the Son of God came to wage against evil is a war that is still being fought. It is being fought both in the life of the world and in our own individual lives. Final victory in this war will mean the complete and utter removal of all evil. It means that we shall live in a kingdom of light where there is no darkness. It also means that we shall be perfectly remade in the likeness of Christ himself. This, according to the New Testament, is God's intention.

> For those God foreknew he also predestined to be conformed to the likeness of his Son, so that he might be the firstborn among many brothers.
>
> Romans 8:29

But it is necessary that Christ not only frees us from sin, but also frees us from death. Death has sometimes been described as the 'last enemy'. The New Testament makes it very clear that when Christ came into the world to fight evil, an essential part of this was the battle to defeat and destroy death. The Book of Hebrews says that Jesus 'tasted death for everyone' (Hebrews 2:9), and that Christ shared our humanity:

> …so that by his death he might destroy him who holds the power of death – that is, the devil – and free those who all their lives were held in slavery by their fear of death
>
> Hebrews 2:14–15

It is perfectly natural to fear death. Shakespeare describes life as a 'brief candle'. Most of us do not want to be snuffed out. When Christ went to the cross, the candle of his life was put out. He was dead, and yet he came back to life. He was like one of those relighting candles which have power to burst back into flame. He himself said:

> The reason my Father loves me is that I lay down my life – only to take it up again. No one takes it from me, but I lay it down of my own accord. I have authority to lay it down and authority to take it up again.
>
> John 10:17–18

Death is like a great barrier of foam used to extinguish the flames when a racing car has caught fire. Jesus went into death. It engulfed him. The flame of his life was extinguished. But he came out the other side alive. He blasted a hole through death.

And the Gospels go further than this. Jesus said, 'Because I live – you shall live also' (John 14:19).

He promised us a part in his own victory over death. He said that if we shared our lives with him – then he would share his life with us. This is the life that conquered death. Jesus promised that we too will burst through death to everlasting life. In the Book of Revelation, John had a vision of Christ saying:

> Do not be afraid. I am the First and the Last. I am the Living One; I was dead, and behold I am alive for ever and ever! And I hold the keys of death and Hades.
>
> Revelation 1:17–18

The New Testament claims that Jesus has the keys that alone can unlock the doors of death and set us free to live eternally in glory. Furthermore, the New Testament sees the defeat of death as resulting not in some shadowy survival in the afterworld, but in our experiencing bodily resurrection akin to that of Christ. Paul tells us that just as we have naturally inherited a body like that of the first human being, so supernaturally we shall one day receive a body like that of Christ, the man from heaven.

> The first man was of the dust of the earth, the second man from heaven. As was the earthly man, so are those who are of the earth; and as is the man from heaven, so also are those who are of heaven. And just as we have borne the likeness of the earthly man, so shall we bear the likeness of the man from heaven. I declare to you, brothers, that flesh and blood cannot inherit the kingdom of God, nor does the perishable inherit the imperishable.
>
> 1 Corinthians 15:47–50

Paul is quite clear that flesh and blood cannot inherit the kingdom of God. Our present earthly bodies cannot live in heaven. One day we shall be given new bodies which cannot decay or die – capable of living in heavenly and eternal realms. We shall be clothed with immortality. The body we receive will be different from the body that we have now. Paul compares the death of our earthly body with the planting of a seed. The seed gives birth to something better.

> The body that is sown is perishable, it is raised imperishable; it is sown in dishonour, it is raised in glory; it is sown in weakness, it is raised in power; it is sown a natural body, it is raised a spiritual body.
>
> 1 Corinthians 15:42–44

We are not told exactly what this new body will be like – but we are told that we shall bear the likeness of Christ, the man from heaven. John's first letter is also very clear that we do not know what that body will be like – but it emphasises that we will be like Christ:

> Dear friends, now we are children of God, and what we will be has not yet been made known. But we know that when he appears, we shall be like him, for we shall see him as he is. Everyone who has this hope in him purifies himself, just as he is pure.
>
> 1 John 3:2–3

Paul also speaks in Philippians of our future body being like Christ's body:

> But our citizenship is in heaven. And we eagerly await a Saviour from there, the Lord Jesus Christ, who, by the power that enables him to bring everything under his control, will transform our lowly bodies so they will be like his glorious body.
>
> Philippians 3:20–21

What a destiny God has chosen for us – to rise in glory, to be conformed to the image of his Son! We shall live in a new world where there is nothing but goodness and where nothing spoils or defiles.

> Praise be to the God and Father of Our Lord Jesus Christ! In his great mercy he has given us new birth into a living hope through the resurrection of Jesus Christ from the dead, and into an inheritance that can never perish, spoil or fade – kept in heaven for you, who through faith are shielded by God's power until the coming of the salvation that is ready to be revealed in the last time.
>
> 1 Peter 1:3–5

The Book of Revelation gives us a glimpse of this new world – but only a glimpse:

> Then I saw a new heaven and a new earth, for the first heaven and the first earth had passed away, and there was no longer any sea. I saw the Holy City, the new Jerusalem, coming down out of heaven from God, prepared as a bride beautifully dressed for her husband. And I heard a loud voice from the throne saying, 'Now the dwelling of God is with men, and he will live with them. They will be his people, and God himself will be with them and be their God. He will wipe every tear from their eyes. There will be no more death or mourning or crying or pain, for the old order of things has passed away.' He who was seated on the throne said, 'I am making everything new!' Then he said, 'Write this down, for these words are trustworthy and true.'

Revelation 21:1–5

Because it is beyond our ability to imagine what heaven will be like, it is pointless to enter into speculation and chase the details. All we can do is to use picture language.

Paul says that God has promised us unimaginable splendour in the world to come.

> No eye has seen
> No ear has heard,
> No mind has conceived
> What God has prepared for those who love him.

1 Corinthians 2:9

Life on earth, at its best, can be very good. Its quality comes chiefly from two things. The first is a great variety of different things to do and experience. The second is other people whom we can love and by whom we can be loved – whose friendship and company we can enjoy and whose lives and joys we can share. The God who gave us this on earth has promised something even better in the world to come. God can give us infinite variety and a quality of deep friendship and love with countless others, and with God himself, which will put this world's relationships into the shade.

Is this too good to be true? Very nearly, but not quite! It is almost too good to be true, yet it is actually true. The Resurrection of Jesus means that we can know that it is true. Just as C S Lewis, when he came to believe that the Resurrection really did happen, was surprised by joy, so too can we be. It really is true that we shall share in the unimaginable splendour of heaven and finally come into the glorious liberty of the children of God, when our earthly bodies become like Christ's body, when we become brothers and sisters of Christ, when we fulfil God's chosen destiny for us, and when we see Christ as he is and bear his image at the last. This is what Paul meant by 'being raised in glory' (1 Corinthians 15:44).

Questions for Discussion

1. Why has the New Testament teaching about the resurrection of our bodies been of such encouragement to Christians throughout the ages?

2. How should we understand the nature of 'spiritual bodies' and 'earthly bodies' as used in 1 Corinthians 15? (It may be helpful to look at the very speculative postscript on p.99 before answering this.)

II

Our Response – Faith and Excellence

How, then, are we to respond to this amazing and wonderful claim that God not only raised Jesus from the dead, but plans that we too will rise from death and be conformed to the likeness of Christ? We have already noted one answer to this question, as it is found in John's first letter.

> Dear friends, now we are children of God, and what we will be has not yet been made known. But we know that when he appears, we shall be like him, for we shall see him as he is. Everyone who has this hope in him purifies himself, just as he is pure.
>
> 1 John 3:2–3

Our response, according to John, is that we should seek to become pure and holy now, because that is what we are destined to be when Christ appears in glory. In other words, we are to begin here on earth what will only be completed in heaven. Paul makes it clear that we are called to be saints (Romans 1:7). The call is serious and it means that we are called to be God's holy people. Here on earth, how can we possibly attempt to become like Christ in any way at all? How can such unpromising raw material be changed into something pure and holy. We know from the New Testament that we are to strive for holiness. But there is a very practical difficulty. How are we, with all our many faults and weaknesses, to make a serious start to become like Christ? One part of the answer is that only God can achieve this. We cannot change ourselves. As Jesus says, 'Without me, you can do nothing' (John 15:5). Only the indwelling Spirit of Christ can make us holy. But there is another part to the answer. It is that we follow Paul's advice to 'work out your salvation with fear and trembling, for it is God who works in you to will and to act according to his good purpose' (Philippians 2:12). Because God is at work in us, and because he has given us enormously rich resources, we must therefore make every effort to become holy. We must work hard at it and strive for holiness. This is the balance between God's part and ours. The second letter of Peter addresses this issue head-on:

> His divine power has given us everything we need for life and godliness through our knowledge of him who called us by his own glory and goodness. Through these he has given us his very great and precious promises, so that through them you may participate in the divine nature and escape the corruption in the world caused by evil desires.
>
> For this very reason, make every effort to add to your faith goodness [excellence], and to goodness, knowledge; and to knowledge, self-control; and to self-control, perseverance; and to perseverance [endurance], godliness; and to godliness, brotherly kindness; and to brotherly kindness, love. For if you possess these qualities in increasing measure, they will keep you from being in-effective and unproductive in your knowledge of Our Lord Jesus Christ. But if anyone does not have them, he is short-sighted and blind, and he has forgotten that he has been cleansed from his past sins.
>
> Therefore, my brothers, be all the more eager to make your calling and election sure. For if you do these things, you will never fall, and you will receive a rich welcome into the eternal kingdom of Our Lord and Saviour Jesus Christ.

2 Peter 1:3–11

In this passage we are given a short, powerful, but comprehensive answer to the question 'How can we begin to become like Christ?' The answer is simple and direct, although it will take the rest of our lives to work it out. But work it out we must, if we are serious about following Christ. Peter insists that we must add to our faith a whole batch of qualities if we are to be effective and faithful as Christians. We must seek to develop them with determination and doggedness. In the next few chapters, we shall examine these qualities one by one. I hope that what I write will encourage readers to think through each step with care and prayerfulness, and to work out in their own lives how they can develop, with God's help, these hallmarks of holy living.

Peter starts with faith. This is the base on which we must build. He assumes that the reader already has faith. What is meant by faith is not just intellectual assent. It means trust – putting our confidence in something. What is that something? It is Christ and what he has done to bring us from death to life. The Apostle Paul argues very strongly in his letter to the Romans that we are put right with God (i.e. justified) by faith. That faith or trust is in all that Christ did through his death and Resurrection to reconcile us to God and bring us the forgiveness of sins.

> For if, when we were God's enemies, we were reconciled to him through the death of his Son, how much more, having been reconciled, we shall be saved through his life.
>
> Romans 5:10

This experience of being put right with God by faith is famously illustrated in *The Pilgrim's Progress*, where John Bunyan gives us a picture of Christian receiving an assurance of sins forgiven, when on his journey he reaches the cross and looks at it in faith:

> Now I saw in my dream, that the highway up which Christian was to go, was fenced on either side with a wall, and that wall was called salvation (Isaiah 26:1). Up this way, therefore, did burdened Christian run, but not without great difficulty, because of the load on his back.
>
> He ran thus till he came at a place somewhat ascending; and upon that place stood a cross, and a little below, in the bottom, a sepulchre. So I saw in my dream, that just as Christian came up with the cross, his burden loosed from off his shoulders, and fell from off his back, and began to tumble, and so continued to do till it came to the mouth of the sepulchre, where it fell in, and I saw it no more.
>
> Then was Christian glad and lightsome, and said with a merry heart, 'He hath given me rest by his sorrow, and life by his death.' Then he stood still a while, to look and wonder; for it was very surprising to him that the sight of the cross should thus ease him of his burden. He looked, therefore, and looked again, even till the springs that were in his head sent the waters down his cheeks

(Zechariah 12:10). Now as he stood looking and weeping, behold, three Shining Ones came to him, and saluted him with, 'Peace be to thee.' So the first said to him, 'Thy sins be forgiven thee' (Mark 2:5); the second stripped him of his rags, and clothed him with change of raiment (Zechariah 3:4); the third also set a mark on his forehead (Ephesians 1:13), and gave him a scroll with a seal upon it, which he bid him look on as he ran, and that he should give it in at the celestial gate; so they went their way. Then Christian gave three leaps for joy, and went on singing,

> 'Thus far did I come laden with my sin,
> Nor could aught ease the grief that I was in,
> Till I came hither. What a place is this!
> Must here be the beginning of my bliss?
> Must here the burden fall from off my back?
> Must here the strings that bound it to me crack?
> Blest cross! Blest sepulchre! Blest rather be
> The Man that there was put to shame for me!'

Bunyan is illustrating Paul's teaching of justification by faith with the words, 'Then he stood a while, to look and wonder; for it was very surprising to him that the sight of the cross should thus ease him of his burden. He looked, therefore, and looked again.'

In a similar way, John Wesley describes in his journal how he came to have assurance of sins forgiven. He describes what happened to him as he listened at a chapel near Aldersgate to a man preaching about justification by faith.

About a quarter before nine, while he [the preacher at Aldersgate Street Chapel] was describing the change which God works in the heart through faith, I felt I did trust in Christ, Christ alone, for salvation, and an assurance was given me that he had taken away my sins, even mine, and saved me from the law of sin and death.

Wesley's emphasis here is on trusting Christ alone for salvation and the change God works in the heart through faith.

More recently, Alec Vidler, sometime Dean of King's College, Cambridge, explains how he came in middle age to understand Paul's teaching on justification by faith:

A turning point or a decisive stage in my attitude to Paul came when at last I saw, or thought I saw, what he was driving at in his teaching about 'justification by faith'.

To put the matter as simply as possible, I now realised – what hitherto I had paid lip service to – that men are incapable of putting themselves right with the all-holy God, or of justifying themselves, by anything that they can do. They cannot save themselves, still less save the world or bring in the Kingdom of God, however hard they try. When Paul said that a 'man is not justified by works of the law but through faith in Jesus Christ', what he said was true, not only of the works or good deeds prescribed by the Jewish Law, but of any conceivable scheme by which men imagined they could perfect themselves and put the world to rights.

Although men are not totally corrupt in the sense that they are incapable of doing any good at all – it would be absurd to say that – the truth is that the best of men and their best accomplishments are tainted or poisoned at the core by their pride or egotism or self-centredness, however fair they may look from outside. I once stated what I believed to be the presupposition of Paul's understanding of Christianity in the following passage:

Christianity ... does not say that, in spite of appearances, we are all murderers or burglars or crooks or sexual perverts at heart; it does not say that we are totally depraved, in the sense that we are incapable of feeling or responding to any good impulses whatever. The truth is much deeper and more subtle than that. It is precisely when you consider the best in man that you see, there is in each of us a hard core of pride or self-centredness which corrupts our best achievements and blights our best experiences. It comes in all sorts of ways – in the jealousy which spoils our friendships, in the vanity we feel when we have done something pretty good, in the easy conversion of love into lust, in the meanness which makes us depreciate the efforts of other people, in the distortion of our own judgement by our own self-interest, in our fondness for flattery and our resentment of blame, in our self-assertive profession of fine ideals which we never begin to practise...

...It came to me with the force of a revelation, that man is basically incapable of saving himself or putting himself right, and that is why it is good news (which is what 'gospel' means) that God sent his Son into the world to save the world, and to give all who will accept the good news a new start in life. For to receive Jesus Christ as Saviour is to be assured that you are made right

> with God … not by anything you can do or by any merits you can
> acquire, but purely as a result of his generous initiative.

We live in an age of doubt – but we need to know that if we put
our trust in Christ's death for us and his rising again for us, then
we are accepted and pardoned and become those who receive his
life and his Spirit. This does, of course, depend on us being
sincerely sorry for our sins and mistakes and being willing with
God's help to seek to put them right. Bunyan, Wesley and Vidler
came to that same assurance by faith.

This assurance will not come for all of us by a sudden
conversion, like John Wesley's. It may be gradual. We may know
that we trust Christ as Saviour and Lord – but we do not know
quite where it started. We may be like Timothy, of whom Paul
says, 'From a child you have known the Scriptures which are able
to make you wise for salvation through faith in Christ Jesus'
(2 Timothy 3:15).

If we are not quite sure whether we have this trust in Christ,
for some it may be helpful to ask in prayer that Christ will be our
Saviour and Lord, and accept with thanks the forgiveness and life
which he won for us through his death and Resurrection. This
may simply be a confirmation of something that is already there.
As has often been said, it is like writing in ink over something that
is already there in pencil – maybe slightly faded.

Alec Vidler has pointed out that faith does not stop there; for
as James says, 'Faith without works is dead' (James 2:26). Paul
says that we are not saved by good works but we are saved *for*
them.

> For it is by grace you have been saved, through faith – and this is
> not from yourselves, it is the gift of God – not by works, so that
> no one can boast. For we are God's workmanship, created in
> Christ Jesus to do good works, which God prepared in advance
> for us to do.
>
> Ephesians 2:8–10

Having established that faith is the basis on which we build,
where are we to go next? The second letter of Peter urges us very
strongly to supplement our faith with excellence. This means the

desire and ambition to be the best that we can be for Christ. For 'excellence' means that we are not satisfied with being second-rate Christians. We really want to become *like Christ* – because that's what we are destined to be one day.

C S Lewis writes in *Mere Christianity*:

> He [Jesus] warned people to 'count the cost' before becoming Christians. 'Make no mistake,' he says, 'if you let me, I will make you perfect. The moment you put yourself in my hands that is what you are in for. Nothing less, or other, than that. You can push me away. But if you do not push me away, understand that I am going to see this job through. I will never rest, nor let you rest, until you are literally perfect – until my Father can say without reservation that he is well pleased with you, as he said he was well pleased with me. This I can do and will do. But I will not do anything less.'

We know from all our experience that if we set low targets we end up with low achievements. Christ sets us the target of perfection. He taught us, 'Be perfect as your heavenly Father is perfect' (Matthew 5:48).

He is well aware that he has put his treasure in earthen vessels. He knows our frailty and weakness. He knows what unpromising raw material we are. But he does intend to fashion us into something very fine and very noble. He loves us and values us. He paid for us with his blood and knows that our eventual destiny is to be like him, as his brothers and sisters. He wants us to learn to walk as he walked. He wants us to take those first faltering footsteps. The Book of Hebrews tells us to take encouragement from the knowledge that a whole host of witnesses to Christ have already taken the same path and finished the course. They have received all that God promised to them that love him (Hebrews 11:32–12:2). The writer urges us, in the light of all that they have achieved, to get rid of everything that stops us running well.

> Therefore, since we are surrounded by such a great cloud of witnesses, let us throw off everything that hinders and the sin that so easily entangles, and let us run with perseverance the race marked out for us. Let us fix our eyes on Jesus, the author and

perfecter of our faith, who for the joy set before him endured the cross, scorning its shame, and sat down at the right hand of the throne of God.

Hebrews 12:1–2

Excellence is about rising to the occasion. We are in very good company. It's about setting our sights high. Our role models, whom we look to and who have set us such a fine example, are the saints who have gone before and who have won the hard-fought fight – and Christ himself. They are our standard. We are like sportsmen playing for the first team and want to play really well – to excel at our sport. In order to do this we are prepared to make sacrifices, to train and work hard to be the best we can be. We are like soldiers who belong to a crack regiment, and we are proud to wear Christ's badge and uniform and wish to carry them with honour.

As Paul said to Timothy, we are to be 'like a good soldier of Christ Jesus … who wants to please his commanding officer' (1 Timothy 2:3–4). This is what excellence is about. It's about our sincere intention to serve Christ well – with his help.

Questions for Discussion

1. Why is it helpful to distinguish between 'intellectual assent' and 'personal trust' when defining the word 'faith'?

2. Why do Wesley and Bunyan lay such stress on Christ's death and Resurrection when they describe their own pathways into faith?

3. In Hebrews 12 (or any other passage of Scripture), what particular incentives are given to encourage us to strive after excellence?

III

Knowledge

After excellence comes knowledge. Why is it so important to put this emphasis on knowledge? Although we may have reached the stage where we are seriously intent on being the best that we can be for Christ, putting this into practice will not be easy. Our old nature is still active. Our minds tend to conform to the world's way of thinking. This is where knowledge comes in. Unless our minds are re-educated and transformed, it will be impossible for us to offer to God the kind of life that pleases him. As Paul puts it in Romans:

> Do not conform any longer to the patterns of this world, but be transformed by the renewing of your mind. Then you will be able to test and approve what God's will is – his good, pleasing and perfect will.

> Romans 12:1–2

Knowledge of God's truth has a vital part to play in the renewing of our minds. A story is sometimes told of a man who had two dogs. The dogs were jealous of each other and fought frequently and fiercely. The man was asked which dog was usually the winner. He replied, 'It's the one I feed the most.' The dogs could be said to represent our two natures – the old and the new. When we become Christians, we receive a new nature. But Paul makes clear in his letters that the old nature is still alive and the two natures are at war with each other. Which one will win? It will be the one we feed the most. Which of our two natures are we feeding? What sort of food are we giving to our souls and minds? What goes into them? What do we think about, listen to, look at and read? Is it the sort of food that will feed the old nature or the new nature? Most of us know from experience that it is very easy to allow our minds to be filled with unhelpful and unhealthy material, the spiritual equivalent of junk food. We are well aware that this does not encourage us in our Christian lives. On the other hand, we are also aware that God has provided food for us which will cause our new natures to be strong and which will renew our minds. Paul, in Philippians, gives us the following advice:

> ...whatever is true, whatever is noble, whatever is right, whatever is pure, whatever is lovely, whatever is admirable – if anything is excellent or praiseworthy – think about such things.

> Philippians 4:8

The Scriptures repeatedly tell us that the words that come from God have great power to purify us, to change us and to lead us to holiness. There are many examples. On the night of his betrayal, Jesus prayed for his disciples, asking God to keep them from evil.

> My prayer is not that you take them out of the world, but that you protect them from the evil one. They are not of the world, even as I am not of it. Sanctify them by the truth; your word is truth.

> John 17:15–17

On the same evening, Jesus had already told his disciples:

> You are made clean because of the word that I have spoken to you.

> John 15:3

Paul making his farewell address to the elders of the Church at Ephesus, gives them his final word of advice:

> Now I commit you to God and to the word of his grace, which can build you up and give you an inheritance among all those who are sanctified.

> Acts 20:32

The Psalms of the Old Testament make the same point. Psalm 119 contains the following claims about the power of God's word to sanctify and purify us.

> How can a young man keep his way pure? By living according to your word.
>
> Psalm 119:9

> I have hidden your word in my heart that I might not sin against you.
>
> Psalm 119:11

If God's word has this sort of power to make us holy, to sanctify us, to change us and to make us more like Christ, then how important it is that we should make time to absorb into our hearts and minds the life-changing word of God in Scripture. Are we prepared to set aside time every day to read the Scriptures? Are we willing to soak up the knowledge and truth that Scripture gives us and to take this exercise seriously? The collect (prayer) from the *Book of Common Prayer* for the second Sunday in Advent explains the process well.

> Blessed Lord, who hast caused all Scriptures to be written for our learning; Grant that we may in such wise hear them, read, mark, learn and inwardly digest them, that by patience and comfort of the holy Word, we may embrace and ever hold fast the blessed hope of everlasting life, which thou hast given us in our Saviour Jesus Christ. Amen.

The truth with which God feeds our hearts and minds does not only come through private reading. Paul, in his letter to the Ephesians, says that Christ gave the Church gifts:

> ...some to be apostles, some to be prophets, some to be evangelists, and some to be pastors and teachers, to prepare God's people for works of service, so that the body of Christ may be built up until we all reach unity in the faith and in the knowledge of the Son of God and become mature, attaining to the whole measure of the fullness of Christ.
>
> Ephesians 4:11–13

41

Are we doing everything we can to make sure that we benefit both in our listening and our reading from the great gifts that Christ has given us of those who teach us God's truth?

Are those of us who have responsibility for teaching and preaching giving food to those who hear and read us – or are we handing out crumbs? Are we feeding Christ's sheep or are the sheep hungry? Paul's advice to Timothy was:

> Do your best to present yourself to God as one approved, a workman who does not need to be ashamed and who correctly handles the word of truth.

2 Timothy 2:15

Are we workers who have no need to be ashamed? Do we take seriously enough the charge which Paul gave to Timothy when he said:

> In the presence of God and of Christ Jesus, who will judge the living and the dead, and in view of his appearing and his Kingdom, I give you this charge: Preach the word; be prepared in season and out of season; correct, rebuke and encourage – with great patience and careful instruction.

2 Timothy 4:1–2

Do we recognise that in both the teaching ministry of the Church and our own private reading of Scripture that the truth of God has the power to cleanse us and make us holy?

It has sometimes been said that if prayer is the Christian's breath, truth is his food. One principal of an Anglican theological college used to warn his students as they left for ordination: 'First you will stop reading. Then you will stop praying.'

Sadly, this has often turned out to be true, as many former students would openly admit. Let us vow, whether ordained or not, that this will not be true of us – that we shall endeavour to feed our new natures and starve the old, so that our minds may be renewed as the Holy Spirit brings the word of God to life for us.

After the Second World War, Germany underwent an intensive programme of denazification. Nazism had infected many areas of society. Because of the Hitler Youth, this was particularly dangerous for the younger generation. Denazification was a programme of complete re-education. Historians differ in their judgement about its immediate effectiveness. But we too need to be re-educated. As Paul says, we must not let the world squeeze us into its mould, but be transformed by the renewing of our minds. This is not the same as brainwashing. We do not think of the German population as being brainwashed in the post-war period. The brainwashing had occurred under the Nazis. We must let the truth of God set us free from the destructive brainwashing of the values of the world. The renewing of the mind is the beginning of the path that leads from a desire to be like Christ to the reality of becoming more like him. It is, of course hard, uphill and probably gradual progress that we shall make.

> You were taught, with regard to your former way of life, to put off your old self, which is being corrupted by its deceitful desires; to be made new in the attitude of your minds; and to put on the new self, created to be like God in true righteousness and holiness.
>
> Ephesians 4:22–24

Questions for Discussion

1. Why are many of us so careless when it comes to the daily discipline of reading the Scriptures?

2. What practical ways can we think of which help us to be more willing to take time to read and pray?

3. There are many reasons for reading the Scriptures. Which, in your opinion, is the most compelling?

IV

And to Knowledge, Self-control

Peter then goes on to urge us to develop self-control. It has been said that self-control is like crossing out the capital 'I' in our lives. It's about deliberately crucifying the sin or habit that 'I' wants to hold on to and which conflicts with what God wants. It is sometimes about giving up something which is not bad in itself for a greater good or something better.

The scene in the Garden of Gethsemane is of Our Lord pleading with his Father that he might not have to drink the cup of suffering, but, with great self-control, accepting that it had to be, for our sake and for our salvation, 'Not my will be done but yours' (Luke 22:42).

We are called upon in Hebrews 12 to follow his example, to throw off everything that hinders us from following Christ and to fix our eyes on him 'who for the joy set before him, endured the cross' (Hebrews 12:1–2).

Christ exercised this self-control knowing that the fruits of his labour would be the satisfaction and the joy of sharing heaven with us. Note his words in Matthew's Gospel:

> Enter through the narrow gate. For wide is the gate and broad is the road that leads to destruction, and many enter through it. But small is the gate and narrow the road that leads to life, and only a few find it.

Matthew 7:13–14

The very running of the Christian race involves self-control – a narrow entrance, a difficult path. The alternative is broad and easy. The alternative to self-control is always easy, but it leads to the wrong place. It leads to destruction.

It is said that wild apes were once caught in Morocco by

putting oranges in large glass bottles which had been cemented to the rocks. The apes were able to put their paws in to the jars and grab the oranges – but the neck of the jars were not wide enough to remove the paws while they were still holding the oranges. Apes would allow themselves to be captured rather than release the oranges. How very foolish! And yet we frequently hold on to things in our lives which are sins or bad habits, or even good things that have become too important to us. We have become addicted to them and refuse to let them go – even when they curtail our freedom and diminish our humanity.

But sometimes we do want to be self-controlled – and sheer weakness stops us. This was true of the disciples in the Garden of Gethsemane. Jesus asked them to stay awake and watch with him. But, exhausted, they fell asleep. As Jesus said, 'The spirit is willing, but the flesh is weak' (Matthew 26:41).

At other times we do not think that it is really all that important to exercise self-control. One of the many areas where this may be true, and in which we find it difficult to exercise self-control, is anger. The letter of James tells us plainly, 'The anger of man does not bring about the righteous life that God desires' (James 1:20). James spends some time in his letter pointing out how often our tongues, when spurred on by anger or bitterness, are uncontrollable. We all know what terrible damage has been caused by us, and sometimes to us, by the uncontrolled tongue. A popular Baptist minister of the last century, called Stephen Alford, used to tell the story of a man who complained that he had a very bad temper and could not get rid of it. Rather foolishly, he said, 'I suppose it's just a cross I have to bear.' The reply came fast and with considerable bluntness, 'It's not your cross. It's your wife's. It's your sin!'

We can see that Stephen Alford was absolutely right. But what about our own sins and bad habits? How many of those do we excuse in a similar way? It was the bad temper that should have been put on the cross. So should all our lack of self-control. The problem for us is that the cross hurts, and hurts very much. That's why Hebrews 12 talks of the sin that clings so closely.

Often, we let bitterness occupy our minds. We sometimes justify this by calling it righteous anger. President Bill Clinton tells how he once asked Nelson Mandela how he dealt with the anger and bitterness that he had been tempted to feel over his long imprisonment and wasted years. Mandela told Clinton that bitterness would have hurt only one person – himself. If he had been bitter and unforgiving, he would have simply prolonged his suffering, by continuing to bear the pain in his mind. Mandela's lack of bitterness and his self-control has enabled thousands of others to come to terms with past injustice and suffering. He has set us all a tremendous example.

Psalm 37 gives us very similar advice to that given by Mandela:

> Do not fret because of evil men
> or be envious of those who do wrong;
> for like the grass they will soon wither,
> like green plants they will soon die away.
> Trust in the Lord and do good;
> dwell in the land and enjoy safe pasture.
> Delight yourself in the Lord
> and he will give you the desires of your heart;
> Commit your way to the Lord
> trust in him and he will do this:
> He will make your righteousness shine like the dawn,
> the justice of your cause like the noonday sun.
> Be still before the Lord and wait patiently for him;
> do not fret when men succeed in their ways,
> when they carry out their wicked schemes.
> Refrain from anger and turn from wrath;
> Do not fret – it leads only to evil.

Psalm 37:1–8

We should note well that we are asked in the Psalm to refrain from anger and are told, 'Do not fret – it leads only to evil.' We have to be reminded constantly that we cannot achieve God's good purposes through bitterness. Now none of this is at all easy for us to grasp and is even more difficult to put into practice.

Another kind of self-control that we often fail to achieve is in the field of ambition. How many Christian lives are ineffective for God because of the overwhelming desire for advancement in status, power or financial reward? Even in the organisation of the churches, Christians long for position and recognition. Sometimes this robs them of fruitfulness for Christ. Jesus, speaking of John the Baptist, said, 'among those born of women there is no one greater than John' (Luke 7:28). John was a truly great man, a man of enormous self-control. He knew that his greatness had to take second place to Christ. John said of Christ, 'He must increase, but I must decrease' (John 3:30). Paul reminds us that as those for whom Christ died the purpose of our lives is no longer to please ourselves but Christ who died for us:

> And he died for all, that those who live should no longer live for themselves but for him who died for them and was raised again.
>
> 2 Corinthians 5:15

There are so many different ways in which we struggle to exercise self-control. We may have to fight long and hard to gain victory. The New Testament, however, is quite clear. We are to make every deliberate effort to put to death the things which we wish to hold on to but which God wants us to relinquish.

> When Christ, who is your life, appears, then you also will appear with him in glory. Put to death, therefore, whatever belongs to your earthly nature; sexual immorality, impurity, lust, evil desires and greed, which is idolatry. Because of these the wrath of God is coming.
>
> Colossians 3:4–6

Repentance means letting go of the sins and bad habits that are so dear to us. In our hearts, most of us know that there is a great deal more of the capital 'I' to be crossed out. We have all made some progress and are better at exercising self-control in some areas of our lives than in others. It is very easy for us to criticise areas of weakness in self-control in other people because we don't think we have a problem with their particular temptation. At the same time we make excuses for our own lack of self-control in other areas.

I recall the story of the dog owner whose pet puppy was allowed to sleep on his bed. At first the dog occupied a small area at the end of the bed. As the puppy developed into a full-grown Alsatian, it took over more and more sleeping space. The pet owner was gradually moved into a smaller and smaller corner of the bed and one night found himself pushed unceremoniously onto the floor – never to be allowed back into the bed! There is a throne in our hearts which is rightly to be occupied by God. We must take great care. When we allow other things onto that throne, they will become idols that take the place of God and threaten the survival of our Christian lives. William Cowper's hymn, 'O for a closer walk with God', makes this point when he writes:

> The dearest idol I have known,
> Whate'er that idol be,
> Help me to tear it from Thy Throne,
> And worship only Thee.

Sometimes, we may be tempted to justify our lack of self-control by saying, 'Well, at least I'm human.' But here we are fooling ourselves and are forgetting that to be truly human is to be like Christ, the second Adam, the proper man. The sin that comes from lack of self-control makes us less like Christ and less than human. It makes us become a shadow of the people we are meant to be. C S Lewis, in his book *The Great Divorce*, tells the story of a coach journey from hell to heaven. Some of the inhabitants of hell are allowed to visit heaven for the day. The creatures from hell are ghostlike figures who are just shadows of their former selves. They have lost much of their humanity. When they get to heaven, they find it too solid, too bright, too real and too painful. But they are allowed to stay in heaven if they will allow themselves to be changed and remade. Nearly all refuse – but one ghost wants to stay. He has the particular sin of lust. This is represented by a lizard which is attached to his shoulder and which keeps whispering obscenities in his ear. An angel tells the ghost that if he really wants to stay he must allow the angel to destroy the lizard. The ghost argues and pleads with the angel that he be allowed to keep the lizard. In the end, after a gigantic struggle to exercise self-control, the ghost agrees to relinquish the lizard. He allows the angel to destroy it. As the angel's hand descends on the lizard, there is a piercing scream of pain from the ghost. The lizard is ripped from the shoulder, crushed and thrown to the ground. The ghost then finds himself slowly transformed into a strong, solid and godlike creature. Then comes the surprise. The lizard, which had been left for dead, revives and is itself transformed into a strong horse, named Desire. The newly changed man climbs onto the horse (now under his control) and rides off into the fields and forests of heaven – a fully formed and perfect human being, recreated in the likeness of Christ, free and in full possession of himself.

I conclude this chapter with two illustrations for our warning and encouragement – one taken from fiction and one from real life. The first is from Graham Greene's novel, *The Power and the Glory*. The novel was set in Mexico in the inter-war period. An anti-Catholic regime was in power which decided to remove and eliminate all priests in some parts of the country. One priest, the chief character of the novel, decided to go underground and defy the authorities. But he was a weak man when under pressure and his inner life deteriorated. He took to drink and became what was known as a 'whiskey priest'. He failed. He was eventually caught and put in front of a firing squad. While waiting for his execution, he reflected on his life and his calling. His sad and silent words were as follows:

> What an impossible fellow I am, he thought, and how useless. I have done nothing for anybody. I might just as well have never lived. His parents were dead – soon he wouldn't even be a memory – perhaps after all he wasn't really Hell-worthy. Tears poured down his face; he was not at the moment afraid of damnation – even the fear of pain was in the background. He felt only an immense disappointment because he had to go to God empty-handed, with nothing done at all. It seemed to him, at that moment, that it would have been quite easy to have been a saint. It would only have needed a little self-restraint and a little courage. He felt like someone who has missed happiness by seconds at an appointed place. He knew now that at the end there was only one thing that counted – to be a saint.
>
> Graham Greene, *The Power and the Glory*

49

As Graham Greene wrote with such powerful effect, 'It would have been quite easy to have been a saint. It would only have needed a little self-restraint and a little courage.' Many of us will feel the sting of these words. Self-discipline is not always that difficult. It often requires just a small adjustment. But we are reluctant to say 'no' to ourselves. And so we miss holiness and we miss 'happiness by seconds at an appointed place'.

The other equally sad but also hopeful illustration is of Jim Elliot, a missionary in Ecuador, who in the 1950s visited a group of head-hunting Auca Indians. He knew it was very dangerous. He and four colleagues were killed with spears. Just before Jim Elliot went on his last journey to meet the Aucas, he was reading from the Gospels the words of Jesus: 'He that holds on to his life shall lose it. He that loses his life for my sake, shall save it' (Matthew 10:39).

He commented on this verse in his diary and wrote the now famous words: 'He is no fool who gives what he cannot keep to gain what he cannot lose.'

What a challenge to self-control!

Questions for Discussion

1. This chapter has given us several examples of lack of self-control. What other common examples can we give from our own experience?

2. What kind of remedies have we discovered for lack of self-control, either in Scripture, the experience of others, or our own experience?

3. Why is lack of self-control so damaging to our own spiritual lives, to our relationships with friends, families and neighbours – and also in the life of the Church?

V

And to Self-control, Endurance

The quality of endurance or perseverance is our next step. Endurance is the dogged desire and capacity never to give up. It is the determination to hold on to the end, no matter what happens. It is the preparedness never to surrender and never to accept final defeat. It sounds like Stoicism, but to the Christian there is a difference. The New Testament promises that those who endure to the end will finally share with Christ in complete and total victory, even though the fight will have been very hard and defeat very close. Those who overcome are promised a victor's crown (2 Timothy 4:8), and Paul encourages us with these words:

> Let us not become weary in doing good, for at the proper time we will reap a harvest if we do not give up.
>
> Galatians 6:9

This talk of triumph and this rugged determination to win is all very well, but in our everyday battle to live the Christian life we often feel powerless and helpless in the face of temptation.

Sometimes it seems that evil is always defeating us. We commit the same sins over and over again and know no victory. How can we conquer that which consistently defeats us? In the following hymn, Isaac Watts pictures the saints who have triumphed over sin and are now in heaven. He also describes their fierce battle with evil while they were here on earth.

> Give us the wings of faith to rise
> Within the veil, and see
> The Saints above, how great their joys,
> How bright their glories be.

Once they were mourning here below,
And wet their couch with tears;
They wrestled hard, as we do now,
With sins, and doubts, and fears.

We ask them, whence their victory came;
They, with united breath,
Ascribe their conquest to the Lamb,
Their triumph to His Death.

They mark'd the footsteps that He trod,
His zeal inspired their breast:
And, following their incarnate God,
They reach'd the promised rest.

Our glorious Leader claims our praise
For His own pattern given;
While the great cloud of witnesses
Show the same path to Heav'n.

Watts was a realist. He knew that the Christian life is not easy. He knew that the battle against evil is a hard one. He said that the saints 'wrestled hard as we do now, / with sins and doubts and fears.'

This great cloud of witnesses knew what it was to be defeated by sin. They had doubts, just as we have doubts. They knew what fear was. But the hymn moves on to tell us how they gained final victory. They ascribed their triumph to the cross.

Watts takes his inspiration in part from chapter twelve of the Book of Revelation:

Then I heard a loud voice in heaven say:

'Now have come the salvation and the power and the Kingdom of our God, and the authority of his Christ. For the accuser of our brothers, who accuses them before our God day and night, has been hurled down. They overcame him by the blood of the Lamb and by the word of their testimony; they did not love their lives so much as to shrink from death.'

Revelation 12:10–11

Here Satan is described as the 'accuser of our brothers', the one who reminds us of our sins and stirs up our guilt so that we feel condemned and hopeless. The passage goes on to say, 'They overcame him by the blood of the Lamb and the word of their testimony and they did not love their lives so much as to shrink from death.'

The point that Watts makes so strongly is that it was Christ's blood which secured the victory. The overcoming was by the blood of the Lamb. They were able to share in Christ's achievement on the cross and finally triumph in their own struggle. To overcome the evil one by the blood of the Lamb means that the saints shared in Christ's triumph over evil by putting their faith in the victory that he had achieved for them on the cross. It means that they were identifying themselves with all that happened at Calvary for them and for their salvation. The key to their victory was their deliberate intention to focus their hearts and minds on Christ's death and his saving work. The deep significance of the Lamb's blood is that by his death Christ won our full salvation. He died for the forgiveness of our sins and he redeemed us from the power of evil. He bought our freedom with his blood. He ransomed us from sin and death. By faith in Christ's blood shed for us, we receive the benefits of his redeeming death. So we need to keep our hearts and minds fixed on this. We need to come frequently to Christ to say thank you for dying for us. Many have found the well-known prayer of St Richard helpful for this purpose.

> Thanks be to thee, my Lord Jesus Christ,
> For all the benefits which Thou hast given me,
> For all the pains and insults which Thou hast borne for
> me.
>
> O most merciful Redeemer, Friend and Brother,
> May I know Thee more clearly,
> Love Thee more dearly,
> And follow Thee more nearly.

In order to keep our minds fixed on the cross, it may be useful to meditate on some writing or music which concentrates on

Christ's passion. A hymn that dwells on the theme of the precious blood of Christ is 'Glory be to Jesus':

> Glory be to Jesus,
> Who, in bitter pains,
> Pour'd for me the Life-blood
> From his sacred veins.
>
> Grace and life eternal
> In that Blood I find;
> Blest be His compassion
> Infinitely kind.
>
> Blest through endless ages
> Be the precious stream,
> Which from endless torments
> Did the world redeem.
>
> Abel's blood for vengeance
> Pleaded to the skies;
> But the Blood of Jesus
> For our pardon cries.

The fourth verse in particular reminds us how effectively the blood of Christ demands our pardon. Sometimes it is good to take verses of Scripture that explore the ideas behind the cross. For example, the Book of Hebrews tells us of 'the sprinkled blood [of Jesus] that speaks a better word than the blood of Abel' (Hebrews 12:24). When Abel was murdered by Cain, his brother, God said to Cain, 'Your brother's blood cries out to me from the ground' (Genesis 4:10). Abel's blood calls out for justice. By contrast, the blood of Jesus cries out for forgiveness. The hymn expresses it well: 'But the blood of Jesus for our pardon cries.'

That blood-bought pardon spells out the defeat of the enemy of our souls and gives us victory over the one who accuses us.

Another great help in claiming the power of the cross in our own lives can be Holy Communion. Two of the many reasons for taking part in a service of communion are to remember and also to proclaim Christ's death. At the heart of the communion service we are deliberately and solemnly identifying ourselves with Christ's death for us. The point of eating and drinking is identification. An illustration of this, which has helped many, is that of wearing a poppy on Remembrance Sunday. The poppy is a moving emblem of men's bodies broken in battle. It grew in profusion on the battlefields of the Western front. The poppy is fragile, like human flesh, and is easily broken and bruised. Its colour is vividly crimson like blood, and stains the earth when crushed. So the poppy is a potent emblem or sacrament of the body and blood of a human being brutally broken in warfare. When we wear a poppy, we wear it on our person to be identified with the suffering of those who died and so acknowledge that it was for us. We also wear it in our hearts and say thank you for their sacrifice.

So it is with the bread and the wine. We take it to identify ourselves openly with Christ's death – with his broken body and shed blood – and in our hearts we say thank you to him for dying for us. We do so with others, so that our identification is open and public. If we think of it like this, we should not be surprised if we are moved. Nor should we be surprised to find ourselves rearmed in the fight against evil.

Christians are sometimes confused about the sacrament and worry about whether they are meant to experience special emotional feelings when receiving the bread and the wine. It might be helpful, instead, that we concentrate our minds on what we are remembering. Our feelings are simply a response to that.

It is important to find time to pray silently immediately before and after taking the sacrament. Hopefully, the service will allow for this. During these times we need to think about Christ's death and how much he loved us and gave himself for us. Perhaps it would be helpful to reflect on the words of a hymn in which the cross is the central theme. This silent prayer is really important. David Hope, formerly Archbishop of York, rightly warned us against what he described as 'wall-to-wall noise' in our services. The point of my emphasising the cross is that the saints overcame evil by the blood of the Lamb, and it is only by coming back to the cross, time and time again, that we will be able to persevere in our fight against sin.

Sometimes we are tempted to think that our faults are so great and our failures so frequent that the struggle is pointless and we might as well give up trying to live the Christian life. We feel that we will never succeed and are doomed to disappoint Christ constantly. John Donne wrestles with this problem of repeated sin. Some have found that the following poem by Donne expresses their own struggle with sin, repentance and forgiveness:

> Wilt Thou forgive that sin where I begun,
> Which is my sin, though it were done before?
> Wilt Thou forgive that sin through which I run,
> And do run still, though still I do deplore?
> When Thou hast done, Thou hast not done;
> For I have more.
>
> Wilt Thou forgive that sin which I have won
> Others to sin, and made my sins their door?
> Wilt Thou forgive that sin which I did shun
> A year or two, but wallow'd in a score?
> When Thou hast done, Thou hast not done;
> For I have more.
>
> I have a sin of fear, that when I've spun
> My last thread, I shall perish on the shore;
> Swear by Thyself that at my death Thy Son
> Shall shine as He shines now and heretofore:
> And having done that, Thou hast done;
> I fear no more.

We must keep coming back to Christ. However many times we fall and however far we fall, he wants us to come to him for forgiveness, healing and restoration. He wants us to go on fighting. Sometimes we shall see nothing but darkness and be in despair. In our darkest hour, he wants us to come back to him, to confess sins and receive forgiveness and start again. Indeed, if we are prepared to come back and start again, we can never be knocked out. It sounds rather Churchillian – but we should make it our solid aim never to give up and never to surrender.

One of our problems may be that we feel that we cannot return to God until we have put things right. But the truth is that we will never put things right until we have come back to God. We need to come just as we are. The restoration process begins with pardon for what we have done.

Toplady put it well in the hymn 'Rock of Ages':

> Nothing in my hand I bring,
> Simply to Thy cross I cling;
> Naked, come to Thee for dress,
> Helpless, look to Thee for grace;
> Foul, I to the fountain fly;
> Wash me, Saviour, or I die.

This emphasis on the efficacy of the cross to deal with our sins is taken up in the popular hymn:

> Just as I am, without one plea,
> But that Thy blood was shed for me,
> And that Thou bidd'st me come to Thee,
> O Lamb of God, I come!
>
> Just as I am, and waiting not
> To rid my soul of one dark blot,
> To Thee whose blood can cleanse each spot,
> O Lamb of God, I come!

In the first verse, the writer points out that there are only two grounds that we have for approaching Christ for forgiveness. The first is that Christ has died for us, and the second is that he bids us come to him. We must come to Christ as we are, with all our unworthiness. It's no use waiting until we are fit to come to him. It is only by coming to him for forgiveness that we shall be made fit.

We have already mentioned the importance of Holy Communion, and such a service may well be an appropriate time to put things right with God. The following words from the *Book of Common Prayer* express finely the balance between our unworthiness and God's great mercy:

> We do not presume to come to this Thy table, O merciful Lord, trusting in our own righteousness, but in thy manifold and great mercies. We are not worthy so much as to gather up the crumbs under thy table. But thou art the same Lord, whose property is always to have mercy: Grant us therefore, gracious Lord, so to eat the flesh of thy dear Son Jesus Christ, and to drink his blood, that our sinful bodies may be made clean by his body, and our souls washed through his most precious blood, and that we may evermore dwell in him, and he in us. Amen.

There is a story told of a Scottish minister distributing the bread and wine at a communion service in the late nineteenth century. He came to one lady who felt that her sins were too great. She called out, 'I'm not worthy, I'm not worthy!' and refused to receive the bread. The reply came in a rather forceful way, 'Take it, woman. Take it! It's for sinners.'

The writer of this book can remember sitting in a Methodist chapel in Cornwall during a communion service, feeling totally unfit to take part, only to hear, to his comfort, the words of an old and saintly minister as he gave out the cup:

> Precious, precious blood of Jesus,
> Ever flowing free,
> Shed for rebels,
> Shed for sinners,
> Shed for thee.

George Herbert's poem, 'Love Bade Me Welcome', deals with the guilty and reluctant soul finding the forgiving love of God.

> Love bade me welcome; yet my soul drew back,
> Guiltie of dust and sinne.
> But quick-ey'd Love, observing me grow slack
> From my first entrance in,
> Drew nearer to me, sweetly questioning
> If I lack'd anything.
>
> 'A guest,' I answer'd, 'worthy to be here.'
> Love said, 'You shall be he.'

'I, the unkind, ungrateful? Ah, my dear,
I cannot look on Thee.'
Love took my hand, and smiling did reply,
'Who made the eyes but I?'

'Truth, Lord; but I have marr'd them; let my shame
Go where it doth deserve.'
'And know you not,' says Love, 'Who bore the blame?'
'My dear, then I will serve.'
'You must sit down,' says Love, 'and taste my meat.'
So I did sit and eat.

We sometimes need a very strong reassurance that Christ will always forgive us and accept us when we come to him in repentance and faith. Scripture gives this reassurance in John's first letter :

> If we claim to be without sin, we deceive ourselves and the truth is not in us. If we confess our sins, he is faithful and just and will forgive us our sins and purify us from all unrighteousness.
>
> 1 John 1:8–9

And in Paul's letter to the Romans:

> Who will bring any charge against those whom God has chosen? It is God who justifies. Who is he that condemns? Christ Jesus, who died – more than that, who was raised to life – is at the right hand of God and is also interceding for us.
>
> Romans 8:33–34

These words are written for our encouragement and we should be comforted by them.

In the light of these assurances, we ought (as many wise teachers have taught) to keep short accounts with God and frequently confess our sins, trusting him for the forgiveness that he offers us through the redeeming blood of Christ. Some words from Colossians which we have already used may help us here:

> For he has rescued us from the kingdom of darkness and brought
> us into the kingdom of the Son he loves, in whom we have
> redemption, the forgiveness of sins.
>
> Colossians 1:13–14

We were rebels – but now we are pardoned. We were exiles – but
now we are members of Christ's kingdom. However amazing it
seems, our sins are forgiven. We should join with Paul in 'giving
thanks to the Father, who has qualified us to share in the
inheritance of the saints in the Kingdom of light'
(Colossians 1:12).

But there is another reason for keeping our eyes concentrated
on the cross. It's not only the means of our redemption and
forgiveness. It is also the supreme example of endurance. In
Hebrews 12 we are encouraged to run the race that is set before
us with endurance:

> Fixing our eyes on Jesus, who for the joy that was set before him
> endured the cross, scorning its shame; and is set down at the right
> hand of the throne of God. Consider him who endured such
> opposition from sinful men, so that you will not grow weary and
> lose heart.
>
> Hebrews 12:2–4

We are to endure because of the example of a host of witnesses to
Christ, who have run this way before us and, above all, because
Christ himself took the same path. We are not alone in our race
and in our battle. We are in very good company. Most of us have
not had to go as far as shedding our blood – so our way is not as
difficult as it was for some of those who went before.

It is probably true that our lack of endurance has a variety of
causes. One of them may be doubt. If we look again at Isaac
Watts' hymn, we note the words:

> They wrestled hard as we do now
> With doubts and sins and fears.

Watts is saying that, like us, the saints had to battle hard with doubt. Doubts can come in various forms. Sometimes, we have genuine intellectual difficulties about particular Christian doctrines or about belief in God or Christ as Son of God. At other times we just feel a lack of certainty and lack of trust in God. This can be caused by tiredness or exhaustion or emotional stress. Many of us have found that grief for a loved one is a great killer of faith. The mixture of mental numbness and actual physical pain that comes with deep grieving is something that eats away at our security and trust. Doubt can be a mixture of the intellectual and the emotional. Grief, for example, may lead to questions about why God allows suffering. A common reaction during grief is to be angry with God. We are angry and bewildered because we feel we are let down.

It is important to realise that doubt is often like a tunnel of darkness and we usually come through. When doubt is caused by personal or emotional upheaval, then we may have to cling tightly to our conviction that the Resurrection of Jesus really happened in historical time – that people actually saw Jesus after his death. Even if we do not feel that Jesus is there, we can hold on to what our intellect tells us to be true. On the other hand, if doubt is intellectual, then it may be appropriate to think hard and long about the evidence for the Resurrection.

I have argued elsewhere that the Christian faith is reasonable. This does not mean that we shall never have doubts. We should not be afraid of doubt or of sharing our doubts with others. We have minds to think and must use them. It is possible for us to have faith even when we have some doubts. For example, we may be frightened of flying and have huge doubts about whether we shall take off or land safely – but that does not stop us making many journeys by air. We board the plane because it is reasonable to believe that it is safe to do so, although we may have some lurking fears for our safety.

At other times our problems with belief may be caused by confusion of mind – partly because we have become too optimistic about the world. As Christians, we do have a cosmic optimism, but we must also be realistic about this world. It is a very messy place, where things go badly wrong. Evil is unfair by its nature and strikes some people more terribly than others. But evil bites at all our heels. No one escapes. Sometimes when a particular sad event hits us, we say that we cannot understand why it happened. We are surprised when we ought not to be surprised. We live in a fallen world. The Creation groans, waiting to be released from frustration and liberated from the bondage of decay (Romans 8:20–21), and brought into the glorious freedom of the children of God. In the here and now, people suffer pain. They cry. They mourn. They die. In the new heaven and the new earth there will be no more death or mourning or crying or pain, for the old order of things will have passed away (Revelation 21:1–4).

'…all things will be well and all manner of things will be well' (Julian of Norwich) – but not quite yet. We must neither be surprised by things going wrong, nor be filled with feelings of self-pity into which we so often sink. We must not imagine that we are going to be exempt from suffering and therefore be unprepared to deal with it when it comes. This is probably where some of us fail most easily and it plays havoc with our faith and Christian life.

Remember the words of Paul:

> For our light and momentary troubles are achieving for us an eternal glory that far outweighs them all.
>
> 2 Corinthians 4:17

and:

> I reckon that our present sufferings are not worth comparing with the glory that will be revealed.
>
> Romans 8:18

Paul goes on to point out that even when everything goes wrong, God is still working out his purpose for us. His purpose is that one day we should be 'conformed to the image of his Son' – to be like Christ, to be his brothers and sisters, entire, complete and perfect. In all our suffering, Paul says that God has chosen our destiny for us and that he chose it long ago and is resolved to carry this out.

> And we know that in all things God works for the good of those who love him, who have been called according to his purpose. For those God foreknew he also predestined to be conformed to the likeness of his Son, that he might be the firstborn among many brothers. And those he predestined, he also called; those he called, he also justified; those he justified, he also glorified.

Romans 8:28–30

How, then, shall we respond to all this? The rest of Romans 8 answers this question and it speaks for itself.

> If God is for us, who can be against us? He who did not spare his own Son, but gave him up for us all – how will he not also, along with him, graciously give us all things? Who will bring any charge against those whom God has chosen? It is God who justifies. Who is he that condemns? Christ Jesus, who died – more than that, who was raised to life – is at the right hand of God and is also interceding for us.

Romans 8:31–34

We have talked a lot about the occasions when, for whatever reasons, be they sins or doubts or fears, we have to hang on to our faith and somehow survive. This is rather like human warfare. Sometimes troops have simply to stand their ground as the enemy throws everything at them. Paul mentions this in the context of Christian warfare when he says in Ephesians:

> Finally, be strong in the Lord and in his mighty power. Put on the full armour of God so that you can take your stand against the devil's schemes. For our struggle is not against flesh and blood, but against the rulers, against the authorities, against the powers of this dark world and against the spiritual forces of evil in the heavenly realms.
>
> Therefore put on the whole armour of God, so that when the day of evil comes, you may be able to stand your ground, and after you have done everything, to stand. Stand firm then...

Ephesians 6:10–14

Four times Paul uses the word 'stand'. Sometimes that is all we can do. Sometimes it will be very grim and very difficult. Endurance means that we stick at it. Sometimes we shall hold on, but only just. Maybe we shall feel like soldiers in a besieged fort waiting for a relief force which never seems to come. Such a situation happened to the US cavalry in the nineteenth century, when soldiers were trapped in a fort by hostile forces. A relief regiment was on the way. When the cavalry were within a certain distance of the besieged camp they were able to signal, 'Hold the fort! We are coming.' Although exhausted and on the point of surrender, the battered soldiers bravely signalled back, 'We will!'

At this time, Philip P Bliss, a Christian songwriter, borrowed this theme to write a popular revivalist hymn:

> Hold the fort for I am coming,
> Jesus signals still.
> Wave the answer back to heaven
> By thy grace, we will.

No analogy is perfect, but another picture which we might find helpful is that of a member of the Resistance movement in occupied Europe during World War II. Life was dangerous and difficult – but collaboration with Nazism was unthinkable. As the struggle became harder, members of the Resistance longed for the day of liberation when the Allies would finally arrive. Sometimes the delay seemed intolerable and it was all they could do to hold on. But then came the day when Allied troops arrived in their town. Liberation had come and they were free for ever from the yoke of Nazism. What a wonderful day! How well worth waiting for!

The New Testament promises that the suffering of Christ's people will not continue for ever. There will come a day when Christ will come again in glory.

The Epistle to the Hebrews comments:

> You need to persevere so that when you have done the will of God you will receive what is promised. For in just a very little while, He who is coming will come and will not delay.

> Hebrews 10:36–37

Paul reminds us:

> The night is nearly over; the day is almost here. So let us put aside the deeds of darkness and put on the armour of light.

> Romans 13:12

However, there is another kind of perseverance, one that involves real advances into enemy territory. We are called to persevere in the work of God. Paul concludes his great passage on the resurrection of our bodies in 1 Corinthians 15 with these words:

> But thanks be to God! He gives us the victory through Our Lord Jesus Christ. Therefore, my dear brothers, stand firm. Let nothing move you. Always give yourselves fully to the work of the Lord, because you know that your labour in the Lord is not in vain.

> 1 Corinthians 15:57–58

We are to be unmovable and persevere in the work of the Lord – because in the Lord our labour is never in vain. Its effects are everlasting.

It is a great antidote to our self-pity, when things go wrong for us, to think of the needs of the human race. There is a world out there in desperate need of help. There is a world without Christ. God has told us to go and make disciples of all nations (Matthew 28:19).

Jesus challenges us powerfully when he asks us to share in the completion of his work:

> 'My food,' said Jesus, 'is to do the will of him who sent me and to finish his work. Do you not say, "Four months more and then the harvest"? I tell you, open your eyes and look at the fields! They are ripe for harvest. Even now the reaper draws his wages, even now he harvests the crop for eternal life, so that the sower and the reaper may be glad together.'

> John 4:34–36

Sometimes we lose sight of this. We forget to be obedient to Christ's command to share the good news. We forget also the sheer joy that can be found in introducing others to our master. We are often pessimistic about the response of the world to the gospel. Christ, however, was very optimistic. He taught that the fields were ripe and ready for harvest. Perhaps we need to rethink our position on this. It could be a great encouragement for our endurance.

But the needs of the world are not just spiritual. Millions are hungry. Millions have no clean water. Millions are needlessly ill. Millions are unnecessarily blind. Millions have Aids. We must not shut our hearts to the desperate plight of so many. When Jesus and his disciples were faced with a large crowd of hungry people, the response of Christ was to say to his disciples, 'You give them something to eat.' They were alarmed and pointed out that all the food they had was a few small loaves and fishes. However, they put these meagre resources into the powerful hands of Christ. He blessed them so that they met the needs of thousands. Maybe this is saying to us that if we put into the hands of Christ what we have and what we are – however feeble and small – he is able to bless it and use this to meet the needs of many, many people.

The war against evil is total and will not end until Jesus returns in glory, when the kingdoms of the world become the kingdoms of our God and of his Christ (Revelation 11:15).

But it is a war against every kind of evil. Injustice, poverty, hunger, oppression and suffering are evils which Christians must fight against. It is true that we ourselves are the battlegrounds over which Christ and the evil one are in conflict. But the societies of the world, as well as the individuals in the world, are also being fought over. That is why the Scriptures command us to be actively concerned with these issues. The argument that we should not get involved in issues of social justice because we can never achieve perfection in this world system is not valid. It would be like arguing that we should not seek to become more like Christ now as individuals because we cannot be perfect this side of heaven. That is why Christian movements have often been at the forefront of relief and medical and educational work. The Salvation Army has been an outstanding example of this. But there is a huge amount to do.

Perhaps we should question ourselves carefully about our attitudes to problems of Third World poverty and the immense human tragedy caused by Aids in sub-Saharan Africa. It is quite legitimate for Christians to argue and disagree about the best way to deal with such needs – but it is not an option for Christians to ignore them. It would be naive of us to believe that we shall succeed in getting rid of all social evils. However, we are not exempt from making every effort to do so, in the same way that we must make every effort to end sin in our personal lives. But we have to accept that these two objectives will only be achieved fully when Christ returns. It is not naive to believe in a sudden and literal return of Christ in glory. There is simply no other way in which the final victory over evil can be won. The New Testament repeatedly promises such an event in which the world system as we know it will be replaced by a new heaven and a new earth. There is no way in which we will, by a gradual process, be able to eliminate all evil from the world. Only Christ's return will make this possible. J B Philips discusses this point in his book, *Ring of Truth*.

We are ourselves somewhere in the vast worldwide vision which Jesus foresaw, and, for all we know, we may be near the end of all things. You simply cannot read the New Testament fairly and come to the conclusion that the world is going to become better and better, happier and happier, until at last God congratulates mankind on the splendid job they have made of it! Quite the contrary is true; not only Jesus, but Paul, Peter, John and the rest never seriously considered human perfectibility in the short span of earthly life. This is the preparation, the training ground, the place where God begins his work of making us into what he wants us to be. But it is not our home. We are warned again and again not to value this world as a permanency. Neither our security nor our true wealth is rooted in this passing life. We are strangers and pilgrims and while we are under the pressure of love to do all that we can to help our fellows, we should not expect a world which is largely God-resisting to become some earthly paradise. All this may sound unbearably old-fashioned, but this is the view of the New Testament as a whole.

Meanwhile, we are called to this great privilege of being co-workers together with all the saints and with Christ himself. What an honour to be his ambassadors! What an encouragement to persevere to the end!

> To him who overcomes, I will give the right to sit with me on my throne, just as I overcame and sat down with my Father on his throne.
>
> Revelation 3:21

Paul was able to say with all sincerity that he had endured to the end, and his words to Timothy are a hard-hitting challenge to our poor service.

> For I am already being poured out like a drink offering, and the time has come for my departure. I have fought the good fight, I have finished the race, I have kept the faith. Now there is in store for me the crown of righteousness, which the Lord, the righteous Judge, will award to me on that day – and not only to me, but also to all who have longed for his appearance.
>
> 2 Timothy 4:6–8

We are all involved in different kinds of work for God. For some it is preaching and teaching; for some it is encouragement; for some the work of prayer. It may be medical work, educational work or relief work, just to name a few. Whatever the sphere of service to which we are called, Paul encourages us to:

> …stand firm. Let nothing move you. Always give yourself fully to the work of the Lord, because you know that your labour in the Lord is not in vain.
>
> 1 Corinthians 15:58

Questions for Discussion

1. Why is endurance such a vital quality for the Christian?
2. What are the most helpful inducements that we can find which will encourage us to fight 'the fight of faith' to the end?

3. What practical things can I do now, or in the future, to help meet the pressing spiritual and physical needs of the world?

VI

And to Endurance, Godliness

Next comes godliness, which is about where our heart is, about what really matters to us, about seeking first God's kingdom and his righteousness. In his letter to the Colossians, Paul speaks of where our hearts should be:

> Since, then, you have been raised with Christ, set your hearts on things above, where Christ is seated at the right hand of God. Set your minds on things above, not on earthly things. For you died, and your life is now hidden with Christ in God. When Christ, who is your life, appears, then you also will appear with him in glory.
>
> Colossians 3:1–4

Godly people are so concerned for God and conscious of the honour of God that they want all that they say and do to bring praise rather than contempt for their Lord. Very much aware as Christians that they bear the holy name, they want to have something of the beauty and fragrance of Jesus in their lives. As ambassadors for Christ, they know that they can bring either honour or dishonour to their king. They hold their master in such reverence that they wish to bring him only honour. This desire comes from an understanding that Christ is utterly and completely worthy of our love, obedience and service. The heart of the godly Christian is at one with the angels who sing:

> 'Worthy is the lamb, who was slain,
> to receive power and wealth and wisdom and strength
> and honour and glory and praise!'

> Then I heard every creature in heaven and on earth and under the earth and on the seam and all that is in them, singing:

> 'To him who sits on the throne and to the Lamb
> be praise and honour and glory and power,
> for ever and ever!'

Revelation 5:12–13

Peter, in his first letter, asks us to revere Christ as Lord in our hearts:

> But in your hearts set apart Christ as Lord.

1 Peter 3:15

Can we honestly say that Christ really has our hearts? Or do they belong to something else?

Godliness is the opposite of worldliness. The question is, 'Who has our heart?' Is it the world or the Father? John, in his first letter, hammers this point home:

> Do not love the world or anything in the world. If anyone loves the world, the love of the Father is not in him. For everything in the world – the cravings of sinful man, the lust of the eyes and the boasting of what he has and does – comes not from the Father but from the world. The world and its desires pass away, but the man who does the will of God lives for ever.

1 John 2:15–17

Who really has your heart? How sad that Paul had to write about his fellow-worker Demas, that he had forsaken him 'having loved this present world' (2 Timothy 4:10). To how many of us are things, money, possessions, status, power and the trappings of this world more important than the Lamb who was slain for us? Where is our heart? Does Christ really dwell there by faith? (Ephesians 3:17)

Jesus taught very simply:

> Do not store up for yourself treasure on earth, where moth and rust destroy, and where thieves break in and steal. But store up for yourselves treasures in heaven, where moth and rust do not destroy, and where thieves do not break in and steal. For where your treasure is, there your heart will be also.

Matthew 6:19–21

It was this deep sense of the honour and the greatness of God that caused Jesus both to submit to his Father's will and to seek to reflect his Father's character. He fervently proclaimed what God had said to Moses, 'You must fear the Lord your God and serve him only' (Deuteronomy 6:13).

It was the same Moses who sought to obey this command who was later held up by the writer to the Hebrews as an example of godliness:

> By faith, Moses, when he had grown up, refused to be known as the son of Pharaoh's daughter. He chose to be ill-treated along with the people of God rather than to enjoy the pleasures of sin for a short time. He regarded disgrace for the sake of Christ as of greater value than the treasures of Egypt, because he was looking ahead to his reward. By faith he left Egypt, not fearing the King's anger; he persevered because he saw him who is invisible.
>
> Hebrews 11:24–27

Moses gave up all that the world had to offer – influence, status, wealth, power and pleasures – because 'he regarded disgrace for the sake of Christ as of greater value'. He saw and revered the invisible God. He honoured God with his whole manner of life.

It is instructive that Moses is described in Scripture as being meek. Meekness and godliness go hand in hand. The prophet Micah challenges us with the words:

> What more does the Lord require of you, but to act rightly and to love kindness and to walk humbly with your God?
>
> Micah 6:8

Godliness is walking humbly with our God. It must be emphasised here that a concern for God's honour does not entitle us in any way to force our beliefs onto others. We cannot *make* people honour God. Godliness comes from the heart and we must not try to bully or browbeat people into faith. The attitude of a godly person is that found in the passage from Peter's first letter that has already been mentioned:

> But in your hearts set apart Christ as Lord. Always be prepared to give an answer to everyone who asks you to give the reason for the hope that you have. But do this with gentleness and respect.

> 1 Peter 3:15

Perhaps, Mother Theresa was one of those who best exemplified that deep desire that our lives should be offered to God as something beautiful and fragrant. Just as parents feel great pleasure when they see in their children the development of real qualities of life and decency, so God takes great delight in seeing his children grow in grace and goodness. Godliness is the concern on our part that our heavenly Father should look at our lives and gain real satisfaction and pleasure. As Paul encourages us, we are to present ourselves as living sacrifices of praise to God (Romans 12:1–2).

This idea of offering of our daily lives to God is summed up for us in the words of Charles Wesley's hymn:

> Forth in thy Name, O Lord, I go,
> My daily labour to pursue;
> Thee, only thee, resolved to know
> In all I think or speak or do.

> The task thy wisdom hath assigned,
> O let me cheerfully fulfil;
> In all my works thy presence find,
> And prove thy good and perfect will.

> Thee may I set at my right hand,
> Whose eyes mine inmost substance see,
> And labour on at thy command,
> And offer all my works to thee.

> Give me to bear thy easy yoke,
> And every moment watch and pray,
> And still to things eternal look,
> And hasten to thy glorious day.

> For thee delightfully employ
> Whate'er thy bounteous grace hath given;
> And run my course with even joy,
> And closely walk with thee to heav'n.

The words 'and run my course with even joy', based on the King James translation of Acts 20:24, remind us that godliness is about finding joy in God and rejoicing in all that he means to us. As the Westminster Confession says, 'Man's chief end is to glorify God and to enjoy Him for ever.' Keeping God at the centre of our daily lives leads to joy in him. This is something we so often miss. Does the life of Christ so possess us that it makes a real difference to the small details of the way in which we conduct our everyday life? Are we so taken up with the greatness and grace of God that we can say with Paul, quite sincerely, 'For me, to live is Christ' (Philippians 1:21)?

Another of Charles Wesley's great hymns addresses this particular issue and helps us to focus our thoughts as we struggle to be Christ-centred. It is a prayer that the Holy Spirit will transform us into godly people.

> O Thou who camest from above
> The pure celestial fire to impart,
> Kindle a flame of sacred love
> On the mean altar of my heart.
>
> There let it for Thy glory burn
> With inextinguishable blaze,
> And trembling to its source return,
> In humble prayer and fervent praise.
>
> Jesus, confirm my heart's desire
> To work, and speak, and think for Thee;
> Still let me guard the holy fire,
> And still stir up Thy gift in me.
>
> Ready for all Thy perfect will,
> My acts of faith and love repeat,

Till death Thy endless mercies seal,
And make the sacrifice complete.

Bramwell Booth, son of the founders of the Salvation Army, used to tell the story of a Salvationist officer who visited the bedside of a dying member of the Army. The dying man pointed to a chest of drawers in his room. In it the officer found a brand-new, unworn Salvation Army uniform. The man explained that he had always been regarded as an odd and strange character by his rather cruel contemporaries. They laughed at him and ridiculed him for his oddness. He had realised that if he wore the uniform, then the ridicule and mockery which he constantly faced in public might be transferred to the Salvation Army and then to Christ, his master. He could not bear the thought of this. Although he wanted to wear the uniform very much, he had not done so, for the Army's sake and for Christ's sake, but he did ask that he might be buried in the uniform. This is a true story and speaks of a godly man who honoured Christ – even to the point of self-denial and hurt. Hebrews 11 gives us a list of such godly people, and concludes:

> Some faced jeers and flogging, while still others were chained and put in prison. They were stoned; they were sawn in two; they were put to death by the sword. They went about in sheepskins and goatskins, destitute, persecuted and ill treated – the world was not worthy of them.

Hebrews 11:36–38

These last words should impress themselves deeply onto our minds: 'the world was not worthy of them'.

Questions for Discussion

1. What would be a good working definition of godliness?

2. Why do we find godliness so difficult to achieve?

3. Are there any practical steps that we can take to become more godly people?

VII

And to Godliness, Brotherly Kindness

The next quality which we are urged to possess in full measure is brotherly kindness. To understand what this means, we had best turn to the one perfect example, Christ himself. The kindness of Christ is shown in that he loved us before we were capable of loving him. As Paul says:

> God commends his love towards us in that while we were still sinners Christ died for us.
>
> Romans 5:8

In other words, Christ loved us and died for us even though we were grubby and very imperfect and quite undeserving of that love. If we would follow Christ's example here, then we must look into his mind to understand his attitude. Paul wrote to the Philippians:

> Your attitude should be the same as that of Christ Jesus: Who, being in very nature God, did not consider equality with God something to be grasped, but made himself nothing, taking the very nature of a servant, being made in human likeness. And being found in appearance as a man, he humbled himself, and became obedient to death – even death on a cross!
>
> Philippians 2:5–8

Paul is expanding a point that he has been making about tenderness and compassion. He has just written:

> Do nothing out of selfish ambition or vain conceit, but in humility consider others better than yourselves. Each of you should look not only to your own interests, but also to the interests of others.
>
> Philippians 2:3–4

He asks us to 'consider others better than yourselves'. We do not think that Paul means that we should consider everybody morally better than we are. He is asking us to consider others more important than we are. They may or may not be more important – but we are to consider them as being so.

This is not easy. But Christ's example is totally clear. Although he was 'in very nature God', he gave up all his importance and status to become a man and to die on the cross. One of the secrets of brotherly kindness is to think of others as people who matter more than we do. We find people irritating, difficult, unpleasant and sometimes impossible. They find us exactly the same. But Paul tells us to think of these same people as those who matter more than we do. How very simple – but how difficult that is! And the only way to achieve it is to keep on remembering that Christ did just that for us.

Christ loved us and gave himself for us because he regarded us as very precious, very dear. If we can think of others as those who were so valuable to God that he sent Christ to die for them, then we may be able to share Christ's loving kindness for other people. If we can go further and picture those same people as they will be one day – perfectly saved and restored through Christ – then we should be able more easily to understand and share his kindness.

The following words, taken from the service of ordination in the *Book of Common Prayer*, should fill us with a deep sense of our responsibility to care for Christ's sheep and to remember how valuable and dear they are to him.

And now again we exhort you, in the Name of Our Lord Jesus Christ, that you have in remembrance, into how high a dignity, and to how weighty an office and charge ye are called: that is to say, to be messengers, watchmen, and stewards of the Lord; to teach and to premonish, to feed and provide for the Lord's family; to seek for Christ's sheep that are dispersed abroad, and for his children who are in the midst of this naughty world, that they may be saved through Christ for ever.

Have always therefore printed in your remembrance, how great a treasure is committed to you charge. For they are the sheep of Christ, which he bought with his death, and for whom he shed his blood.

No one in Christian service can take these words lightly. A very practical way of dealing with our lack of kind feelings towards people is to try to wish them well and to pray for their good. Ask God to bless them and pray specifically that things will go well for them. It may be good for us to do some act of kindness for them, or give some present to them. This is hard work when we dislike people or feel that they have wronged us or have wronged someone we know. Forgiveness is not easy – because it means accepting the hurt caused. But if we pray for someone's welfare and happiness and salvation, it is much easier to forgive. We cannot pray for someone's eternal pardon and not forgive them ourselves.

The Book of Hebrews tells us to 'consider how we may spur [or provoke] one another to love and good deeds'. Instead, we so often provoke each other to irritation and anger. Paul, in his letter to the Romans, lays down an important principle of brotherly kindness. He is writing about the problem of whether or not it was permissible and wise to eat certain foods or keep special days. Paul writes:

> If your brother is distressed because of what you eat, you are no longer acting in love. Do not by your eating destroy your brother for whom Christ died.

> Romans 14:5

He continues in Romans 14:21, 'It is better not to eat meat or drink wine or to do anything else that will cause your brother to fall.' If we are showing brotherly kindness, then we shall not want to do anything that hurts another or does not build them up. Paul concludes:

> We who are strong ought to bear with the failings of the weak and not to please ourselves. Each of us should please his neighbour for his good, to build him up. For even Christ did not please himself, but, as it is written: 'The insults of those who insult you have fallen on me.'

> Romans 15:1–3

Just as Christ did not please himself, so we are 'to please our neighbour for his good.'

This is an important point to make here. We are asked to do as Christ did. The emphasis is on our pleasing our neighbour *for his good*. 'For his good' means that we are genuinely interested in his welfare. Just as a good parent will pursue the interests of his child, but not at the expense of others and not to the point of spoiling his offspring, so we will seek to build up our neighbour. This may sometimes mean giving tough or unwelcome advice. It does not mean spoiling someone by giving in to every selfish whim. The good parent or schoolteacher does not do that. It is not kind, for example, to give a large bag of sweets to a three-year-old child just before mealtimes. Nor is it kindness to give money to a drug addict if we know that it will be spent on feeding his habit. It is not kind to give in to eccentric or self-centred demands, if by doing so we make someone worse rather than better. We are seeking to build up, not to pull down into a mire of self-indulgence of self-pity. Sometimes, Jesus had to be very tough with his disciples. Note well his interview with Peter by the lakeside after the Resurrection. He gave Peter a rough ride – but for Peter's own good and to build him up (John 21:15–22).

If we are stir up one another to 'love and good works', then we need to think of practical ways of doing this. An encouraging letter at the right time can be really helpful to our Christian growth. How often has the giving or lending of a particular book changed someone's life? It may be that, without being interfering or patronising, we can talk naturally to other Christians about the ups and downs of our spiritual lives. We might be able to pinpoint things that have been helpful to us. So many Christians seem to regard this kind of conversation as almost bad taste; but if we never talk about our inner lives, we are missing out on a whole area of possible encouragement for others. Do we really have a genuine desire that our fellow believers may know God more deeply and shine more brightly for him? If so, we shall take the whole business of encouragement very seriously as a responsibility of our brotherly love. We shall also take seriously our responsibility to pray regularly for others. We shall want to pray about their problems and the things that matter to them. We shall want to pray that they will become mature and Christlike people. Furthermore, we shall persist in this prayer and not give up easily. It may be instructive to see how Jesus prayed for the disciples (for example in John 17), or how Paul prayed for the New Testament Christians (for example, in Ephesians 1:15–23; Philippians 1:3–11 and Colossians 1:9–12). It may be useful to base our prayers on these passages, noting what sort of things Jesus and Paul prayed for. These passages certainly deserve our prayerful and thorough study. What matters is that we really do care about the quality of the lives of our brothers and sisters in Christ, and that we commit ourselves to pray frequently for them that 'they might be filled with all the fullness of God'.

But there is a wider application of this quality of brotherly kindness. Like Christ, we must have compassion for the multitude and weep over Jerusalem. We cannot look at the suffering of the world and be indifferent. We must respond. Our responsibility to show kindness is not just towards friends and immediate neighbours. It is towards the whole human race. Jesus taught that our neighbour is everybody. If the people next door were hungry, we would feed them. If people are starving in the Third World, we often harden our hearts or perhaps send a small donation. Children are going blind for want of a small sum of money, and yet we remain indifferent. We think of ourselves as kind people. Who is kidding whom?

At the end of Mary Batchelor's biography of Catherine Bramwell-Booth (granddaughter of the founder of the Salvation Army) there is a delightful postscript:

> On 3 October 1987 Catherine Booth was, in Army language, 'promoted to glory'. Her life spanned the years from the first mustering of the Salvation Army to the present day, and her passing marks the end of the beginning of that great movement in which for so many years she was a potent influence.
>
> Among her letters, written to past students at The Army's Training College, is one different in character from the rest. In it, Catherine the mystic takes over from the practical, commonsense adviser. She describes in 'The Law of the Forest', a wood where she sat, watching the trees and listening to the wind, and of the strange instinctual knowledge of far-off happenings that came to

her. She heard a tall pine tree, lamenting its fate as guardian of the wild things of the wood against the buffeting of wind and storm, when it could have been carved into a thing of beauty in its own right. 'How long?' it sighed. Then the ancient oak, standing firm and unmoved, delivered to the other trees the law of the forest. 'The glory of the tree,' said the oak, 'is to give shelter rather than receive it; to protect … to nourish, to uphold … to hold its roots in every storm for the comfort of all other creatures, until … the service is completed.'

Catherine was true to the law of the forest. Her glory, and the glory of her family, was to stand firm, to give strength and succour to those too weak or unprotected to withstand the storms of life. Now 'the service is completed'. The glory of serving others has been transformed into the glory of heaven, where 'his servants shall serve him, and they shall see his face … and there shall be no night there.'

from *Catherine Bramwell-Booth* by Mary Batchelor[1]

The prophet Micah (6:8) asks of us that we should act rightly and love kindness and walk humbly with our God. Note that we are to love kindness. Catherine Booth radiated kindness.

But now we move on to the last quality which Peter urges us to possess, that of love. As with all the other qualities, there is much overlap, and it is difficult to distinguish an absolute difference between brotherly kindness and love.

Questions for Discussion

1. Where are our main areas of failure when it comes to showing brotherly kindness?

2. How might we take practical steps to become more genuinely kind people?

3. Why does this kindness matter so much to God?

---

[1] Mary Batchelor, *Catherine Bramwell-Booth*, Lion Publishing, 1986

VIII
And to Brotherly Kindness, Love

The love mentioned in 2 Peter 1 takes us beyond even brotherly kindness. It is our love for, and devotion to, our master. It is the love that we can have because God loved us before we loved him. It is the love that loved us while we were still rebels. Paul writes:

> God demonstrates his own love for us in this: While we were still sinners, Christ died for us.
>
> Romans 5:8

As John says, it is the love that caused God to send Christ to die for us:

> This is how God showed his love for us, he sent his one and only Son into the world that we might live through him. This is love; not that we loved God, but that he loved us and sent his Son as an atoning sacrifice for our sins.
>
> 1 John 4:9–10

It is the love that drove Christ to take up the cross.

> It was just before the Passover Feast. Jesus knew that the time had come for him to leave this world and go to the Father. Having loved his own who were in the world, he now showed them the full extent of his love.
>
> John 13:1

Our love is a reflection of that love and a response to it. It is devotion to God which is owed to him because he is both our maker and redeemer.

A story is sometimes told of a small boy called Harry, who was very talented at woodcraft. He decided to build a small model boat. He spent months of his time and all his pocket money designing and making the boat. When Harry had finished, the model was very fine and gave him great pleasure. He very much enjoyed sailing it on a nearby stream. But one day, after heavy rain, the stream was in flood and the boat got carried away and was lost. The boy was heartbroken. He felt that he had lost something of himself. He really grieved for his boat. Some weeks later, walking past a shop in a local neighbourhood, he spotted what looked like his boat in the window. He ran in and asked the shopkeeper if he could have a look at the model. On inspection, Harry realised that the boat was the one that he had made. The shopkeeper was very sympathetic when he heard the boy's story – but said that he had paid money for the boat and could only return it to the boy if he paid for it. The shopkeeper did, however, agree to keep the boat for the boy provided that Harry could collect enough money within three months. The next twelve weeks were spent by the young child earning as much money as he could from odd jobs and by saving every penny of his pocket money and every gift of money he received. After a really difficult time, Harry had enough money to go to the shop and buy back the boat. He walked out of the shop with the purchase in his hands and spoke these words: 'You are mine. You are mine twice over. You are mine because I made you and you are mine because I bought you at great expense.'

We can all guess whom the boy is meant to represent. It is Jesus. We are the boat. We belong to Christ – firstly because he made us and secondly because he bought us back when we had got lost – he bought us with his blood.

> You are not your own. You were bought with a price.
>
> 1 Corinthians 6:19–20

> For you know that it was not with perishable things … that you were redeemed … but with the precious blood of Christ, a lamb without blemish or defect.
>
> 1 Peter 1:18–19

We keep returning to the cross. We need to keep going back there to see that love and feel its power – power that will pull us away from the idolatry of putting other things on the throne of Christ. I have already suggested that a useful way of fixing our minds and hearts on Christ's death for us is to use poems and hymns for prayer and meditation and to take time to read them thoughtfully. I have found the following hymns helpful. They are taken from an old hymn book, and each one refers to a different aspect of the cross. The first example, by William D MacLagan, explores the implications of the words exchanged between Jesus and the dying thief who was crucified at his side. The words 'remember me' are repeated several times, and the hymn becomes a personal prayer that we can use today. The language may be a little quaint, but the message is deeply challenging.

> 'Lord, when Thy kingdom comes, remember me';
> Thus spake the dying lips to dying Ears;
> O faith, which in that darkest hour could see
> The promised glory of the far-off years!
>
> No kingly sign declares that glory now,
> No ray of hope lights up that awful hour;
> A thorny crown surrounds the bleeding Brow,
> The hands are stretch'd in weakness, not in power.
>
> Yet hear the word the dying Saviour saith,
> 'Thou too shalt rest in Paradise today';
> O words of love to answer words of faith!
> O words of hope for those who live to pray!
>
> Lord, when with dying lips my prayer is said,
> Grant that in faith Thy kingdom I may see;
> And, thinking on Thy cross and bleeding head,
> May breathe my parting words, 'Remember me.'
>
> Remember me, but not my shame or sin;
> Thy cleansing blood hath wash'd them all away;
> Thy precious death for me did pardon win;
> Thy Blood redeem'd me in that awful day.

Remember me; yet how canst Thou forget
What pain and anguish I have cause to Thee,
The cross, the agony, the bloody sweat,
And all the sorrow Thou didst bear for me?

Remember me, and, ere I pass away,
Speak Thou th'assuring word that sets us free,
And make Thy promise to my heart, 'Today
Thou too shalt rest in Paradise with Me.'

The second example, by Cecil Alexander, takes the words of Jesus on the cross, 'I thirst'. It deals with the irony of an event in which the one who made all the water in the world was thirsty. The hymn then links Christ's physical thirst with the deep longings of his heart – that we should be saved for ever. Lastly, we are asked to respond with our own spiritual thirst for Christ.

His are the thousand sparkling rills,
That from a thousand fountains burst,
And fill with music all the hills;
And yet He saith, 'I thirst.'

All fiery pangs on battlefields;
On fever beds where sick men toss,
Are in that human cry He yields
To anguish on the cross.

But more than pains that rack'd Him then,
Was the deep longing thirst divine
That thirsted for the souls of men:
Dear Lord! And one was mine.

O Love most patient, give me grace;
Make all my soul athirst for Thee;
That parch'd dry lip, that fading face,
That thirst, were all for me.

We need to realise just how much we owe to Christ and how great our debt to him is. The woman who anointed Jesus was forgiven much and therefore loved much (Luke 7:47). We have all been forgiven a very, very great deal. The debt of love we owe to Christ is beyond calculation.

A few years ago, just after a forest fire had destroyed areas of California, some local people were picking their way through the burnt-out remains of a smallholding. They came across the charred body of a hen. One of them turned the body over with a stick. From underneath the body emerged three live chicks. During the course of the fire, the hen had protected her offspring by gathering them under her body and wings. The fire had killed the hen but her chicks were saved. We can take this as a picture of Christ dying on the cross to save us. As Paul says:

> God made him who had no sin to be sin for us, so that in him we might become the righteousness of God.
>
> 2 Corinthians 5:21

How do we even begin to pay back to Christ this debt of love? Perhaps the following hymn, by Ernest Hardy, helps us to express our heartfelt desire to respond to his love.

> O dearest Lord
> Thy Sacred hands
> Were pierced by nails for me.
> O pour Thy blessing on my hands
> That they might work for Thee.
>
> O dearest Lord
> Thy Sacred feet
> With nails were pierced for me
> O pour Thy blessing on my feet
> That they might run for Thee.
>
> O dearest Lord
> Thy Sacred head
> With thorns was pierced for me

> O pour Thy blessing on my head
> That I might think for Thee.
>
> O dearest Lord
> Thy Sacred heart
> With spear was pierced for me
> O pour Thy Spirit in my heart
> That I might live for Thee.

We need to understand too that God's love goes on and on. It is without limit. As Paul says:

> He that did not spare his own Son, but gave him up for us all – how will he not also, along with him, graciously give us all things?

Romans 8:32

Richard Baxter, a great Christian teacher of the seventeenth century who exercised a remarkable ministry in Kidderminster, wrote in his book, *The Saints' Everlasting Rest*, these challenging words:

> Reader, stop here and think a moment what a state this is. Is it a small thing in your eyes to be loved by God – to be the son, the spouse, the love, the delight of the King of glory? Christian, believe this, and think about it: you will be eternally embraced in the arms of the love which was from everlasting, and will extend to everlasting – of the love which brought the Son of God's love from heaven to earth, from earth to the cross, from the cross to the grave, from the grave to glory – that love which was weary, hungry, tempted, scorned, scourged, buffeted, spat upon, crucified, pierced – which fasted, prayed, taught, healed, wept, sweated, bled, died. That love will eternally embrace you.

Questions for Discussion

1. For you personally, what is it that is most likely to lead you to respond to God's love? Is there some piece of writing or teaching that has led you to love God more?

2. How do you distinguish between genuine love and mere emotionalism?

IX

Short-sightedness

We have so far looked in some detail at 2 Peter 1. We have traced Peter's argument from verses three and four. He begins by telling us that God has called us to share in his divine nature and to escape from this world's corruption. He makes it very clear that God has given and promised all that is necessary for us to achieve this end.

Peter urges us, in the light of all God's promises to us, to work very hard at adding to our faith a list of qualities which include excellence, knowledge, self-control, endurance, godliness, brotherly kindness and love. He explains that these qualities will make us effective and fruitful in our relationship with Christ. He then concludes:

> If you do these things, you will never fall, and you will receive a rich welcome into the eternal kingdom of Our Lord and Saviour Jesus Christ.
>
> 2 Peter 1:10–11

So why is there a problem? Why are we so lacking in these qualities? If we are honest, most of us will admit that our attempt to develop these qualities is extremely patchy. In reality we are half-hearted about it and just do not grasp the urgency or see the importance of getting this right. The reason, or at least a major part of the reason, for this is to be found in Peter:

> If anyone does not have [these qualities], he is short-sighted and blind and has forgotten that he has been cleansed from his past sins.
>
> 2 Peter 1:9

The writer of the letter suggests that there is a very real problem of inner or spiritual blindness – or failure to see and to understand *spiritual reality*. Paul takes this idea very seriously. In his second letter to the Corinthians, he says that 'the god of this age has blinded the minds of unbelievers, so that they cannot see the light of the gospel of the glory of Christ' (2 Corinthians 4:4).

And the blindness is not confined to unbelievers. The failure to grasp spiritual reality is part of our condition as fallen creatures. It's like the effects of a sea mist that keeps coming in. It prevents us from seeing out clearly and it keeps coming back – sometimes unexpectedly.

It is interesting that Paul refers to the evil one as 'the god of this age'. It is perfectly true that we often find the brightness of this world's passing glory so completely dazzling that we are blind to the urgency and importance of the things of God. As in the parable of the sower, 'the deceitfulness of riches and the cares of this world' are choking our Christian lives and stunting our spiritual growth. This is happening to many of us on a daily basis, and often continues month in and month out. It may result in years of fruitless discipleship.

Sometimes we live as Christians with something that can only be described as a bunker mentality. We behave and think as if this passing order of things was permanent. But Christ has promised that this world will someday pass away. A new order and new rule will be established. Do we behave as if the old regime is going to last for ever? Like the small group of senior Nazis who, in early 1945, shared Hitler's bunker, ignoring outside events and continuing to uphold their beliefs, do we refuse the inevitability of change? Do we adhere to the old world's standards? Are we still impressed by its tatty grandeur? Do we fail to recognise that a new rule, a new authority, a new set of values will shortly be in place and that the old will have gone for ever?

One high-ranking Nazi felt deeply thrilled and honoured when Hitler made him head of the German Red Cross in late April of 1945. He was a war criminal. The honour was temporary and meaningless, but the man concerned was so blinded by Hitler's remarkable powers of influence that his grip on reality had gone. These people in the bunker lived in an unreal world – a shadowland (as C S Lewis might have said). The real world was about to happen with the Allied victory in early May 1945. In the same way, there will be a future moment when 'the kingdoms of this world become the kingdom of Our Lord and of his Christ' (Revelation 11:15), and the old order will have disappeared for ever.

Do the trappings and the tinsel and the empty glory of this world so grip our minds and hearts that they weaken our allegiance to the king who is coming? The old revivalist hymn asks that we may be reminded of the story of Christ's love. One verse begins:

> Tell me the same old story,
> When you have cause to fear
> That this world's empty glory
> Is costing me too dear...

We are in serious danger of coming close to idolatry. We are exchanging the eternal God for idols of earthly prestige, wealth, success and pleasure. Most of the time we do not even see what we are doing. The 'god of this age' has been very successful. The prophet Jeremiah spoke strongly to Israel in a similar situation:

Has a nation ever changed its gods? (Yet they are not gods at all.) But my people have exchanged their Glory for worthless idols.

'Be appalled at this, O heavens, and shudder with great horror,' declares the Lord.

My people have committed two sins: they have forsaken me, and the spring of living water, and they have dug their own cisterns, broken cisterns that cannot hold water.

Jeremiah 2:11–13

It was 'love of the present world' that caused Demas to forsake Paul (2 Timothy 4:10) and John's first letter pleads with us: 'Dear children, keep yourselves from idols' (1 John 5:21).

Part of our problem, as Peter suggests, is that we have forgotten that we have been cleansed from our old sins. We have lost that first thrill and joy that we used to have. We have ceased to be amazed at the saving love of Christ. As the young Church in

Ephesus was warned, we have lost our first love (Revelation 2:4).

How then are we, as short-sighted Christians, to deal with this blinding mist that our enemy sometimes sends? One clear answer must be the example of Paul of using prayer, praying that God will clear the mist, penetrate the darkness and open our eyes to see.

In the first chapter of Ephesians, Paul describes how he prays for Christians at Ephesus. He asks God to give them a spirit of wisdom and revelation, that they may know God better and that the eyes of their hearts may be enlightened in order that they may know the hope to which he has called them, and also the power that God has for them – the same power that raised Jesus from the dead (Ephesians 1:17–20).

The three reasons why Paul prays that they will receive inward clarity of vision are, firstly, to know God better; secondly, to understand and know the future hope of glory to which God has called them; and, lastly, to understand and know the Resurrection power which can change them and enable them to live new lives for God.

There are so many occasions when we need to ask God directly to clear our spiritual sight. If we feel that the enemy is too strong for us, we need to pray as Elisha did when surrounded by hostile forces. The story is told in the second book of Kings:

> 'Go, find out where he is,' the king ordered, 'so that I can send men and capture him.' The report came back: 'He is at Dothan.' Then he sent horses and chariots and a strong force there. They went by night and surrounded the city.
>
> When the servant of the man of God got up and went out early the next morning, an army with horses and chariots had surrounded the city. 'Oh, my lord, what shall we do?' the servant asked.
>
> 'Don't be afraid,' the prophet answered. 'Those who are with us are more than those who are with them.'
>
> And Elisha prayed, 'Oh Lord, open his eyes so that he may see.' Then the Lord opened the servant's eyes, and he looked and saw the hills full of horses and chariots of fire all round Elisha.

2 Kings 6:13–17

We need our eyes opening to the vast resources of God that he puts at our disposal in the fight against evil. The same applies even when we read the Scriptures. Here, we need to pray with the psalmist, 'Open my eyes that I may see wonderful things in your law' (Psalm 119:18).

When we have times of prayer, quietness and meditation, we may need to ask first that God will pierce the mist and break through the cloud. We can pray with Paul in Ephesians, that we may have power to grasp how wide and long and high and deep is the love of God and to know that love (Ephesians 3:18–19).

It is also important that we ask God to enable us to have a clear vision of the glory that he will share with us in his eternal kingdom. Unless we really grasp that we are destined to live one day in utter splendour, we shall not be able to get the small things of this life in perspective. Sometimes we get obsessed with the trivial. We can all be very petty and miss the big important picture. We are often small-minded and get upset about little things that have no long-term importance. We need to understand our future in order to put the present in its right place.

One rather quaint poem from Victorian days makes the point very well:

> One day of days,
> One dawning yet to be
> I shall be clothed
> With immortality.
>
> And on that day
> I shall not greatly care
> That Jane spilt candle-grease
> Upon the stair.

But sometimes our blindness is so severe that we have ceased to realise that something has gone seriously wrong. We have drifted into easy-going complacency about our spiritual state. The letter to the church in Laodicea in the Book of Revelation speaks of this:

> You say, 'I am rich; I have acquired wealth and do not need a thing.' But you do not realise that you are wretched, pitiful, poor, blind and naked. I counsel you to buy from me gold refined in fire, so that you can become rich; and white clothes to wear, so that you can cover your nakedness; and salve to put on your eyes, so that you can see.
>
> Revelation 3:17–18

The message is blunt. Christ is waiting to respond to our penitent prayer for spiritual riches, clothing and eye salve (so that we can see). Christ is banging away at the door of our lives and we do not even see that he is there. He wants us to enjoy his love and friendship. Sincere and honest prayer is what he calls for. These verses are written for believers. They apply to us! Christ is there waiting for our invitation to make again the personal and life-saving contact that opens our eyes, cleanses and renews us and thaws us out of our coldness and indifference. We may start by asking him for the ability to see again.

My conclusion is this – the god of this age constantly attempts to prevent us seeing clearly that Christ has redeemed us, forgiven us, empowered us and has destined us to be like him. We must take spiritual blindness seriously and address it by direct appeal to God to clear the mists. If we do this often, we shall find the battle easier to fight and see more clearly the stages that we must pass through on the road to holiness.

Peter then closes this section in verses 10 and 11:

> Therefore, my brothers, be all the more eager to make your calling and election sure. For if you do these things, you will never fall, and you will receive a rich welcome into the eternal kingdom of Our Lord and Saviour Jesus Christ.

Once more, he wants us to do all we can do to develop these qualities. If we do, he promises, we will receive a rich welcome into Christ's kingdom and we will never fall.

This is the way, he writes, in which we make our calling and election sure. Many Christians spend a lot of time arguing about the mechanics and the process of election. The purpose of election in Scripture is to tell us that God intends to bring us to the goal he has chosen for us. We should not, therefore, get hung up on the process. We are elected to bear fruit (John 15:16), to do good works (Ephesians 2:10) and to holiness (Ephesians 1:4). We are elected to eternal life (Acts 13:48) and to be adopted as sons of God (Ephesians 1:5). We are elected to be conformed to the likeness of Christ (Romans 8:29).

Election is about both the destiny of glory to which God has called us and also the pathway we must take to get there. If we start to be Christlike here on earth, then we are confirming that we are on our way to becoming the perfect people we shall be in heaven. If we are to be like Christ in heaven, then we need to begin on earth what will only be one day completed in heaven. If we do these things, says Peter, we shall receive a very warm welcome into Christ's eternal kingdom.

This is meant to spur us on. To face Christ on that day and to hear him say, 'Well done!' will be worth more to us than any other praise we have ever been given.

Those who honour me, I will honour,' says the Lord.

1 Samuel 2:30

On this note, I include a light-hearted but touching poem written by Vachel Lindsay. It is about the reception given to General William Booth, founder of the Salvation Army, as he is pictured entering heaven and meeting his master face to face.

> Booth led boldly with his big bass drum
> (Are you washed in the blood of the Lamb?)
> The Saints smiled gravely and they said:
> 'He's come.'
> (Are you washed in the blood of the Lamb?)
> Walking lepers following, rank on rank,
> Lurching bravos from the ditches dank,
> Drabs from the alleyways and drug fiends pale –
> Minds still passion-ridden, soul-powers frail:
> Vermin-eaten saints with mouldy breath,
> Unwashed legions with the ways of death –
> (Are you washed in the blood of the Lamb?)

Every slum had sent its half-a-score
The round world over. (Booth had groaned for more.)
Every banner that the wide world flies
Bloomed with glory and transcendent dyes.
Booth died blind and still by faith he trod,
Eyes still dazzled by the ways of God.
Booth led boldly, and he looked the chief,
Eagle countenance in sharp relief,
Beard a-flying, air of high command
Unabated in that holy land.
Jesus came from out of the court-house door,
Stretched his hands above the passing poor.
Booth saw not, but led his soldiers there
Round and round the mighty courthouse square.
Then in an instant all that blear review
Marched on spotless, clad in raiment new.
The lame were straightened, withered limbs uncurled
And blind eyes opened on a new sweet world.
Drabs and vixens in a flash made whole!
Gone was the weasel-head, the snout, the jowl!
Sages and sibyls now, and athletes clean
Rulers of empires, and of forests green!
The hosts were sandaled, and their wings were fire!
(Are you washed in the blood of the Lamb?)
But their noise played havoc with the angel-choir.
(Are you washed in the blood of the Lamb?)
Oh, shout salvation! It was good to see
Kings and princes by the Lamb set free.
The banjos rattled and the tambourines
Jing-jing-jingled in the hands of queens.
And when Booth halted by the curb for prayer
He saw his Master thro' the flag-filled air.
Christ came gently with a robe and crown
For Booth, the soldier, while the throng knelt down.
He saw King Jesus. They were face to face,
And he knelt a-weeping in that holy place,
Are you washed in the blood of the Lamb?

Of course, it is true that, as Paul says in 1 Corinthians 13, we shall only receive perfect sight in Christ's glorious kingdom.

> Now we see but a poor reflection as in a mirror; then we shall see face to face. Now I know in part; then I shall know fully, even as I am fully known.

> 1 Corinthians 13:12

This very beautiful German hymn of Paul Gerhardt (translated by Robert Bridges), suggests that only at death will we be able to see everlasting reality absolutely clearly – just as the removal of sunlight at night-time enables us to see vast areas of starlit space:

> The duteous day now closeth,
> Each flower and tree reposeth,
> Shade creeps o'er wild and wood:
> Let us, as night is falling,
> On God our Maker calling,
> Give thanks to him, the Giver good.
> Now all the heavenly splendour
> Breaks forth in starlight tender
> From myriad worlds unknown;
> And man, the marvel seeing,
> Forgets his selfish being,
> For joy of beauty not his own.
> His care he drowneth yonder,
> Lost in the abyss of wonder;
> To heaven his soul doth steal:
> This life he disesteemeth,
> The day it is that dreameth,
> That doth from truth his vision seal.
> Awhile his mortal blindness
> May miss God's loving kindness,
> And grope in faithless strife:
> But when life's day is over
> Shall death's fair night discover
> The fields of everlasting life.

Questions for Discussion

1. To what extent is spiritual short-sightedness or blindness a real problem for Christians today? Can you think of examples of this from your own personal experience?

2. The chapter mentions some possible remedies for such blindness. Are there other remedies which you have found in Scripture, from the experience of other Christians or in your own Christian life?

Postscript

Speculation, Speculation, Speculation

1. The Resurrection of the Body – Its Nature

The exact nature of our new body is not clearly spelt out in the New Testament. But Paul writes in Philippians that it will be like Christ's glorious body:

> …who by the power that enables him to bring everything under his control, will transform our lowly bodies so that they will be like his glorious body.
>
> Philippians 3:21

It seems that Paul is here making a comparison with the body Jesus had after his Resurrection. This ties in with his claim in Corinthians that 'just as we have borne the image of the man of earth – so we shall bear the image of the man from heaven'.

John's first letter repeats this idea: 'We do not know what we shall be – but when he appears we shall be like him because we shall see him as he is.'

What our future existence and substance is to be is far from clear – but the New Testament is clear that it will be 'glorious' and beyond all that we can now imagine.

> No eye has seen, no ear has heard, no mind has conceived what God has prepared for those who love him.
>
> 1 Corinthians 2:9

To say that we shall be like Christ does not mean that we shall be replicas and copies of him. We shall be brothers and sisters of Christ – not identical twins. But it may well mean that our bodies will have the same properties as Christ's Resurrection body. In the Gospels, Jesus is able to slip in and out of our three-dimensional world. Will that be possible for us also?

It is worthwhile noting that some of the speculation going on in the world of modern physics is viewing the dimensions of space and time in a much more fluid way.

It is often said that there should be a total ban on any philosopher or theologian going anywhere near quantum physics. However, Keith Ward (formerly Regius Professor of Divinity at Oxford), wrote a fascinating and highly speculative article in *The Tablet* (April, 2005). He attempts to see resurrection in the light of modern physics. He argues that for many people:

> ...the idea of a bodily resurrection of Jesus has become an absurdity, and the idea of life after death a mere fantasy. Partly this is because modern science seems to show the total dependence of the mind on the brain, and suggests that consciousness is just a by-product of material processes, and could not exist without them.
>
> Actually, the picture given by modern science is more complex. Quantum physics has undermined materialism – one major quantum physicist, John von Neumann, said, 'All real things are contents of consciousness', and the idea of electrons as small solid particles has been rejected in favour of a form of reality more mysterious and perhaps unimaginable.
>
> Moreover, modern physicists propose ideas far removed from classical materialism. Freeman Dyson, in an influential paper on the far-future universe, has proposed that human thoughts and feelings might ultimately be downloaded into magnetic fields composed of clouds of photons and gravitons, long after galaxies and stars have ceased to exist, if the universe continues to expand in a linear way...
>
> These may seem extreme views ... The astonishing thing is that they take seriously the possibility, from a strictly scientific point of view, that we might come to exist in very different forms, even in different sorts of space-time, in another universe and long after the death of our physical bodies...
>
> If, in the light of this, we ask what happened to the body of Jesus, it becomes plausible to think that his body always was, like all physical bodies, an appearance to human minds of a deeper unimaginable reality. It could be instantaneously transformed

into another form (a 'spiritual body', Paul calls it) in another space-time. That is a contemporary and scientifically feasible way of thinking of the 'ascension' or 'assumption' of a body into heaven.

The unique thing about Jesus' transformation would be that his transfigured body appeared in solid physical form, for short and intermittent periods, for some time after his death.

Keith Ward, 'The Quantum Leap',
The Tablet, 2 April 2005, p.9

2. The Resurrection of the Body – Dimensions

Another often quoted piece of speculation is the attempt to imagine what it would be like for a two-dimensional person (should one exist) to try to understand the idea of three-dimensional life. The following may help us to understand the problems we have in imagining more than three dimensions. It was probably first used in the late nineteenth century by a mathematician called Edwin Abbott who produced a book called *Flatland*.

We begin by trying to imagine a person who is two-dimensional. Here is a cartoon drawing of a person called Henry. He knows what up and down are and forwards and backwards – but he does not experience or understand the concept of sideways. He is flat against a wall. He is two-dimensional.

Then we introduce John, who is a three-dimensional person. However, he has the ability to lose one of his dimensions. He decides to flatten himself against the wall and meet Henry.

John then explains to Henry that he, John, is usually three-dimensional but has given up one dimension to meet Henry. Henry says that he does not believe that there are more than two dimensions. John persists in his claims, and Henry challenges John to prove that he is usually three-dimensional. John agrees and walks away from the wall sideways and regains his third dimension. As far as Henry is concerned, John simply disappears.

John then reappears. He pursues his argument further and draws a square around Henry.

He then gets Henry to agree that John can only get to Henry if he crosses one of the four lines of the square. John then moves away from the wall and comes back to Henry inside the square – but without crossing the four lines.

Henry has to admit that although he cannot conceive of more than two dimensions, John may have a point – if he is able to disappear to somewhere else and then reappear.

We will now apply this illustration to the Resurrection of Jesus. We examine the possibility that the body of Jesus after his Resurrection was able to exist not only in our three-dimensional world, but also in a reality in which dimensions are different.

All this, of course, is only speculative and proves nothing. It might, however, help us to glimpse a part of what actually happened to Jesus.

According to the Gospels, Jesus appeared to his disciples on the evening of his Resurrection day. He was suddenly there inside a locked room with them. Jesus was physically present and, according to Luke's account, told them that he was not a ghost because he had flesh and bones. He asked them for something to eat to show that he was physical. He invited them to touch him. All this happened and yet he had entered the room without coming through the door. A three-dimensional room has six sides. If there are more than three dimensions, then there is a way into a room which does not involve entry by one of the six sides – just as there was a way into Henry's square for John which did not involve crossing Henry's four sides.

How would all this apply to Jesus and the empty tomb? Looking at things this way, the reason why the stone had been rolled away was not to let Jesus *out*. It would be to let the disciples *in* – so that they could see that Jesus had gone. If Jesus was resurrected with new properties which transcended our three-dimensional limitations, then there would have been a way out of the grave clothes, headband and tomb which did not mean passing through them. They were all wide open – just as Henry's square was wide open to John.

Seen in this light, the Ascension of Jesus described in Acts might be less difficult to imagine. Jesus had appeared to and disappeared from his disciples several times after his Resurrection for a period of about six weeks. When he wished to make it clear that he was going for the last time, he needed to do something that would convince his followers that the appearances were at an end. His last goodbye was dramatic. He left them from the Mount of Olives, moving upwards – until a cloud took him out of sight. According to this explanation, Jesus did not speed off into space. He waited until he was out of sight and then stepped out of our three-dimensional world, leaving them the promise that one day he would return in the same way that they had seen him go.

As I have already said, this is all very speculative; but most physicists today would accept that there are many more than three dimensions and most agree that there are probably eleven. I am not qualified to judge, but leave this interesting speculation as it stands – to amuse, puzzle or possibly enlighten.

3. Resurrection of the Body – the Problem of Time

There has been much debate in the past about the exact connection between our old earthly bodies and our new resurrection bodies. There is a clear promise, in both 1 Corinthians 15 and 1 Thessalonians 4, that those who are alive when Christ returns in glory will instantly be transformed when that event occurs. But what is supposed to happen to those who die before the event? Do they hang around in some sort of waiting room? Are they conscious or unconscious? Some have argued that, in this in-between time, they exist as a memory held in the mind of God, and that at the final resurrection God will recreate them.

There are two obvious objections to this idea. The first is that what is recreated may be exactly like us, but it is not us. Reproduction furniture may be exactly like the original, but it is not the original. I want to be the original person that I was, not a copy, even an exact one. What constitutes a person? I would want to argue that continuity – not just of memory, but of substance – is a vital ingredient of personhood.

This brings us to the second objection. The New Testament does not suggest that when we die we are just a memory in the mind of God until the final resurrection. St Paul said that to die meant to be with Christ, which is far better. This suggests some kind of happy conscious existence at the very least. In other words, we continue to exist substantially after death. The fact that that substance is not the same as the physical matter of our present three-dimensional world does not mean that it does not exist. Spirit is not the same as matter, but it still has substance. For example, Christians have always claimed that Jesus was 'of one substance with the Father'. It is always risky for philosophers and theologians to get involved in the arguments of modern physics – but it is still fair to note that physicists are seriously debating possibilities of universes beyond our own where time, space and even substance behave in ways that would have seemed impossible to scientists of a few decades ago.

Some now question the very existence of time. The Bible claims that with God time is very different from time as it is on earth.

> With God, a day is like a thousand years and a thousand years like a day.

> 2 Peter 3:8

Is it not possible that when we die and leave this present time system, we shall find ourselves arriving in God's time at the final day of resurrection, together with all those who have died at different earthly times? Maybe time will be so different in the world to come that the question of time gaps and waiting rooms becomes meaningless.

All this speculation about the nature of the world to come is fascinating. It can of course be helpful, if it enables us to get our imaginations around difficult concepts. But, in the end, it is only speculation – only guess work, which lacks any certainty.

What is really important is that God has revealed more certain truths to us through his Son and through the Scriptures. These truths are what I have sought to write about in this book – that God chose to rescue Adam's helpless race by sending us a new Adam. This new or second Adam would, by his life, death and resurrection, save the human race and restore human beings to divine glory – by forgiving their sins and remaking them to be like him. I have argued that God has poured the immense resources of heaven into this loving and saving act. It is therefore of the utmost importance that we respond with urgency and sincerity to this most gracious initiative. This response means turning away from all that we know to be wrong and putting ourselves into the hands of the one who alone can make us fit to dwell with God.

I believe that 2 Peter 1 is a challenging and life-changing passage of Scripture. I pray that those who study it will be changed by it. I finish with the words of Peter:

> His divine power has given us everything we need for life and godliness through our knowledge of him who called us by his own glory and goodness.

2 Peter 1:3

Acknowledgements and Permissions

My thanks go to Peter Cole who has worked tirelessly to enable this book to be reproduced.

Text from Evelyn Waugh, *Brideshead Revisited: The Sacred and Profane Memories of Captain Charles Ryder*, Penguin Classics, 1999, © Evelyn Waugh reproduced by permission of Penguin Books Ltd.

Text from Graham Greene, *The Power and the Glory*, Vintage, 2005 reproduced by permission of David Higham Associates.

Mere Christianity by C S Lewis, copyright © C S Lewis Pte. Ltd. 1942, 1043, 1944, 1952. Extract reprinted by permission.

Text by Winston Churchill reproduced with permission of Curtis Brown Ltd, London, on behalf of The Estate of Winston Churchill. Copyright Winston S Churchill

Text from Malcolm Muggeridge and Alec Vidler, *Paul: Envoy Extraordinary*, copyright © 1972 Malcolm Muggeridge and Alec Vidler, reproduced by permission of Harper Collins. Copyright in the customised version vests in Athena Press publishers.

Extract from Keith Ward, 'The Quantum Leap', *The Tablet*, 2 April 2005 reproduced by permission of *The Tablet*, http://www,thetablet.co.uk

Printed in Great Britain
by Amazon